## What People Are Saying about Healing the Heart and Joan Hunter

In this day and time when women are juggling how best to secure their place in the home, the workplace, and in the body of Christ, this incredible book, authored by Joan Hunter, offers a God-inspired road map. Joan's clarity of purpose and commitment to doing the will of God in the face of adversity and circumstance rings out loud and clear from the opening page, all the way through to the final paragraph. A must-read for all women from various ethnic backgrounds, denominational affiliations, and strata of society! Through the Holy Spirit, Joan has provided us a powerful, life-changing book designed to bless any and every one who reads it.

**—Vivian Berryhill**
President and Founder,
National Coalition of Pastors' Spouses
www.pastorspouses.com

Everyone…absolutely *everyone*…has experienced a "dark time" and wondered when—or *if*—it would ever end. Joan Hunter knows that feeling all too well. In *Healing the Heart*, she shares the pain of marital betrayal and the shocking discovery that her own husband was gay. This book doesn't pull any punches; it's an honest, revealing account of how one woman arose from deep despair to live in ultimate victory. Read her story and find triumph for yours!

**—Marilyn Hickey**
Founder and President of Marilyn Hickey Ministries

Joan Hunter is an amazing blend of strength and vulnerability. It is impossible to read her story without being inspired, challenged, and encouraged. *Healing the Heart* is a must-read for everyone who is experiencing crisis in their marriage, health, or finances. Joan overcame all of these and now reveals how she did it. Her book is a catalyst for conquering defeat.

Col
Get

D1017674

Wow! This new book by Joan Hunter will change your life. In this powerfully transparent and real-life testimony you'll be moved beyond words as you read how she overcame unthinkable circumstances through the healing power of forgiveness. Joan shares that Jesus Christ is the source of all our physical, mental, and emotional healing. Not only does she reveal the need for us to get free but unlocks key strategies of how we and our families can get free from our circumstances and stay free. This book is a must-read for all who work as counselors or advisors and for those who find themselves in similar circumstances. **—Jeff Jansen**
Evangelist / Revivalist
Founder of Global Fire Ministries

Awesome! From the very onset of *Healing the Heart*, there is the ever-painful reminder of the horrendous effects of betrayal. Closeted homosexuality, also known as *living on the downlow*, is a destructive, cancerous spirit that often leaves families disillusioned, devastated, and ultimately destroyed. But thanks be unto God—not Joan Hunter, nor her children. Not only does Joan passionately give her readers the intimate details of her journey to restoration and healing, but she also gives insightful principles for the same healing anyone can receive—a supernatural healing from God—a healing of the heart! **—Pastor Michael A. Stevens, Sr.**
Author of *Straight Up: The Church's Official Response to the Epidemic of Downlow Living*

What a joy to see the Lord's powerful redemption in Joan's life! Because she has overcome, she now has a deep well of compassion and anointing from which to minister to broken people. Read on...these pages will inspire you to arise from your ashes and see what God will do with your redeemed life! **—Melva Lea Beacham**
Director of International Development,
Christian Friends of Israel-Jerusalem

# Joan HUNTER

OVERCOMING BETRAYAL
IN YOUR LIFE

# the Healing HEART

WHITAKER
HOUSE

## HEALING THE HEART:
## Overcoming Betrayal in Your Life

Joan Hunter
526 Kingwood Drive Suite 333
Kingwood, TX 77339
www.joanhunter.org

ISBN-13: 978-0-88368-130-5
ISBN-10: 0-88368-130-7
Printed in the United States of America
© 2007 by Joan Hunter

Whitaker House
1030 Hunt Valley Circle
New Kensington, PA 15068
www.whitakerhouse.com

**Library of Congress Cataloging-in-Publication Data**

Hunter, Joan, 1953–
Healing the heart : overcoming betrayal in your life / Joan Hunter.
p. cm.
Summary: "Shows that God wants to give you emotional and spiritual healing as well as physical healing, and deals with recovering from betrayal"
—Provided by publisher.
ISBN-13: 978-0-88368-130-5 (trade pbk. : alk. paper)
ISBN-10: 0-88368-130-7 (trade pbk. : alk. paper) 1. Suffering—Religious aspects—Christianity. 2. Spiritual healing. 3. Hunter, Joan, 1953– I. Title.
BV4909.H755 2007
248.8'6—dc22                    2006039537

3  4  5  6  7  8  9  10  11  12  **UJ**  14  13  12  11  10  09  08  07

# Dedication

This book is dedicated to my four wonderful daughters,
Charity, Spice, Melody, and Abigail.
If it were not for them and the grace of God,
I would not be here today.
When I thought I had no reason to stay on this earth,
they gave me reason to live—them!
I love them more than words can say. The Word says,
"Children are a gift from God"!
They truly are my gifts from Him!

# Acknowledgments

Naida Johnson, RN, CWS, FCCWS, for her devotion to this
book. A special thank-you for the many hours she spent in
the compiling and editing of this book.

Special thanks to my friend Bill Johnson for his help with
the cover of this book. It truly shares my heart,
that God heals and cleanses our hearts through the
washing of the water of the Word, as it says in
Ephesians 5:26, *"That He might sanctify and cleanse
her with the washing of water by the word."*

# A Note from Joan

*Since we all interpret situations through our previous individual experiences, other people involved in my life may view the specific details a little differently than I have shared within these pages.*

*In this book, I have shared from my heart about how I felt during this time. Within the following chapters, you will read about my fears and my pain, as well as my victories as I share how God brought me through.*

*And He can and will bring you through, too!*

*—Joan*

# Contents

# Foreword

One night, I got home late, went straight upstairs, and got ready for bed. Following my usual routine, I had my prayer time with the Lord and read my Bible.

From my "personalized" *Living Bible*, Exodus 13:3 reads, "Then God said to Joan, *'This is the day to remember forever—the day of leaving Egypt and your slavery; for the Lord has brought you out with mighty miracles.'*"

I thought that was an absolutely awesome Scripture. I received exactly what God wanted me to receive. Just that one Scripture gave me peace beyond anything I could have imagined. And I thought, *God, You brought me out of slavery. Now I can share this with others, and You will bring them out of bondage. You will bring them out of slavery.*

This verse should be yours to claim as your own after you finish this book. You will be able to claim it and expect the mighty miracles He has waiting for you.

Know that He is waiting for you as well as for me. He has great things in store for each of us. Why? Because He is our Father. He loves each and every one of us.

# Introduction

On September 9, 2003, I had the privilege of going to The Master's Touch Church just outside Orlando, Florida, to hear Mark Chironna. At the end of the service, he called me out to prophesy over me. He knew I was Charles and Frances Hunter's daughter (he had ministered with them years ago), but that was all he knew.

We had never met before that day. He laid his hands on me and began to weep, overwhelmed with compassion.

He said, "My God, my God, the pain...the pain that you have been through."

It was as if my pain had been transferred into him. I understand now what that feels like, because when I pray for people sometimes God lets me feel their pain. (I am able to pray with greater compassion with this overwhelming feeling.)

He was crying, "The pain. The pain."

I said, "Yes, I have been through hell."

Then he said, "You had to go to hell to get the keys to help open the doors for others to get healed from their own hell." He continued on with an incredible prophetic word about the calling of God on my life, and did I ever need to hear that word from the Lord.

Within the pages of this book are the keys that God gave me to help set you free of the pain of the past.

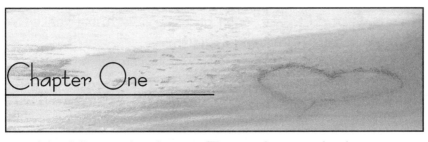

# Chapter One

# When Your Darkest Hour Lasts Longer than Sixty Minutes!

I got home from work to discover a message on the cell phone. What I heard sent me into a total state of shock. I began to shake as confused thoughts whirled through my head.

*Did I hear him right? Did the message really say what I thought it said? Or am I trapped in a nightmare? God, please let this be a bad dream. This can't be happening...not after twenty-five years. Not again.*

I had forgiven him once, years before. I didn't understand why then, and I didn't understand now. All I could think was, *What did I do? What didn't I do? I love him. Wasn't that enough?*

Besides my own pain, I had to think about what our children would say and how this would affect them. I knew they would be devastated. He was not just their dad—he was their pastor. And then there was the question of how we would make it financially.

We had grown up together. If anyone had asked, I would have told them we were each other's best friend. But best friends don't do this to each other. I gave him twenty-five years of my life. How could he do this?

God help me! What should I do?

Who else knows about this? Who else was involved with him? How long has this been going on?

He had been a pastor for eighteen years. What would our church friends and previous members say? Had he approached anyone in the church? He had counseled numerous people throughout the years. What did he tell them? How could he help others while he himself was doing this? How did he keep it so well hidden? What were they going to think now? What were they going to say? They were going to be so disappointed. They were going to think we were pretending to serve God. But I wasn't pretending. I really wanted to serve God and minister to His people with my whole heart. How could he be doing those horrible things while ministering at church under the pretense of being a fine, godly man? All the messages that he gave about a godly marriage and the marriage covenant, were they all lies?

All those years we traveled around the world with Mom and Dad. In his betrayal, there was a potential of hurting their worldwide ministry. What would they do? They trusted him implicitly and this is how he acted. He was living his dream of ministering, singing, and traveling around the world, but at whose expense? I couldn't believe it was true.

I thought he loved me. I thought he loved the girls. How long had this been going on? How much of our marriage was a sham? How much of it was a lie? Will I ever know? Will I ever understand? Will I ever feel good again? How will I make it? Will I ever laugh again? Will God ever use me again to do anything for Him? I just want to die.

I had no idea what was going to happen next. I depended on him for everything. I didn't know how I was going to survive financially with three of the girls in college. I needed him. How could I face another day, another moment? My whole life revolved around him. Where could I go now? What was I to do without him? He could do everything. He taught me how to cook, to decorate the house, to do everything. He was my identity. Without him, I was nothing.

My life was devastated, ripped apart at the seams, shredded into nothingness. I was afraid to face life alone. I would have no husband to help me, love me, or hold me. No one to walk with, talk with, or share things with. I have never liked being alone. How would I cope? Our girls were older and leaving home to start their lives on their own.

My heart hurt, my chest ached, and my head pounded. I couldn't see through my tears. My arms and legs didn't want to work. I know I should eat, but the thought of food or drink nauseated me. Every system in my body was screaming, "Stop the pain!"

Who could I talk to? Who would understand the pain I was feeling? No one! I recalled so many hurting people that I had counseled through the years. Was this the pain they felt? No, they couldn't possibly have felt the stabbing, throbbing pain I felt throughout my body. Every cell hurt, every inch. I wasn't sure I wanted to take another breath. I didn't want to open my eyes. I didn't want to see the empty house, the empty space in the bed where he used to sleep. Everything I looked at screamed his influence, his plans, his creative talents, him!

I couldn't stop all these thoughts from running through my mind. I was a completely different person from the day before. That instant in time had shaken my world and my identity to the core. What happened to the smiling, happy, cheerful Joan? When I looked in the bathroom mirror, the person staring back was not the same person who used to look back at me. The person I had become had a puffy face and blank, dead eyes staring at nothing. She reeked of failure, pain, agony, frustration, worthlessness, desertion, and devastation. She was not beautiful, but ugly. She looked like a poor, lost soul who was more dead than alive. Yesterday's Joan would love her, encourage her, and pray for her. Somebody needed to help her, but I just couldn't do it. I couldn't help anyone anymore. I felt dead inside. My heart had been ripped out, and my life had fallen apart.

> My heart had been ripped out, and my whole life had fallen apart.

In the next few days, the phone seemed to ring off the hook. I couldn't answer it. I didn't want to talk to anyone. Most of the calls were from people whom he had hurt, wanting to tell me something terrible about him, something that he had done to them. I had no answers for the people who were calling. They were just adding to my pain. All I could do was cry. *Phone, please stop ringing!*

I told myself that somehow I had to be strong. But how could I, when I felt weaker than a newborn kitten? I had no strength. I knew nothing would ever be the same again. My whole world had changed. My whole life had fallen apart.

Not only my life, but the girls' lives, too. They would have so many questions. How could I even begin to answer them? I didn't know. I was so afraid for them as well as for myself.

I tried to put on a mask and hide what was happening. But makeup wouldn't cover up the hurt inside. I had hid behind the mask of smiles and laughter before, when others hurt me, but this time was different. I couldn't even fake a smile. *Maybe I can smile again someday. I just don't understand what went wrong.*

In the days that followed, I tried to figure out how I could have fixed our marriage. But always the thoughts came back: *Who am I kidding? There was no way I could have satisfied him and his desires, but how could he do this to his children? He loved them so much. He loves me....No, he loved me....No, he never did. What is the truth?*

I kept remembering what he had said. *It was all an act. He said he was just a very good actor. Our marriage was just a front. He was using me and our marriage to hide his real feelings and his secret life. Was our life together a sham, nothing, worthless? Did it mean anything to him? I was just another rung on his ladder toward his ultimate goal. Was I just being used? I was a convenient presence in his façade of the ideal Christian family portrait. A portrait he could obviously walk away from without regret.*

I knew I was going to lose the house. I couldn't possibly pay for it. On my income, I couldn't even maintain the utilities. He certainly wasn't going to take care of me anymore. This house had been my haven, my nest, for over eighteen years. How could I turn my back on it and leave? The memories, the fun we had here. The children grew up in this house. Our friends and family gathered here weekly for great Christian fellowship. The laughter and joy of excited children, church members, and Christian friends from around the globe echoed through the halls. Our beautiful house. And now it was so silent. Except for the sound of my uncontrollable sobbing.

Oh, how dumb I was! I was so blind. Why couldn't I see what was really going on? I believed all his lies. Even when I questioned him, he was so good at making excuses, and I was so gullible that I believed him. The house, the bills, the children, our friends, the dog...oh, no, the dog. She adored him with blind devotion. She was always his dog. How was she going to survive his leaving her?

I pleaded with God, Please, let this be a bad nightmare! Let me wake up and cry for joy because my life is so close to perfect and normal! Please let my family still be intact and following our dream of working in the ministry together and serving God, hand in hand, throughout our lives.

He was out there feeling nothing for ripping apart the home we built together. He thought what he had done was okay. He could see nothing wrong. How could we be so close yet so far apart? What of the last twenty-five years was real?

All I felt was pain! I had to do something, but what? My reason to live was gone. I lived to serve and please him all these years. Our children were grown and didn't need me. I knew they could make it without me. I didn't really have any reason to get up anymore. I didn't want to fight anymore. I felt like hell had surrounded me, and there was no exit. I wanted to go to sleep and not wake up to another day of this pain and fear.

I knew I couldn't survive crying all day and all night. I had no strength, no hope, and no energy. I didn't know how to get out of this very dark, very deep pit of despair. It would be so easy to just die right now and not have to face another minute, another person, another phone call, or our children. I didn't want to deal with the pain of my physical body, the emotional torment raging through my mind, or the spiritual questions of "Why, God, why?" I knew I should talk to someone, but who could possibly help me or know what I was experiencing? Nobody could. My life was a mess, and I was falling apart. I had lived with a lie and now I had to bear the pain.

I feared that the whole world would know what was wrong with me and my marriage. They would look at me with contempt, hatred, or pity. They would know I failed. After all was said and done, I was still that worthless, stupid, ugly person who had done nothing right since birth. My biological father had abandoned me and now my husband had abandoned me. All those voices from long ago were right. I was not worth anything to anyone. I had been used and now thrown away like an old shoe.

## "God, help!"

# Chapter Two

# The Bomb

Twelve years earlier, before that awful night, as my husband and I were leaving for another Healing Explosion, our daughter Melody had said, "Are you leaving us again for God?" The Holy Spirit spoke through her that day. We had to make some adjustments. The Holy Spirit had already been dealing with us to give more of our attention to "our family," meaning both our church family and our four daughters. He didn't say He was done with our traveling in ministry; however, He did say we needed to make an adjustment to bring the traveling into a more appropriate balance.

Working with my mom and dad, Charles and Frances Hunter, at their large meetings throughout the United States and several other countries was exciting and very rewarding. People were getting healed and saved. We were doing great things for God, and Mom and Dad needed both of us to help them during these events. There were so many details. We both had vitally important parts to play in the coordination and completion of the Healing Explosions that were touching so many people's lives.

Our time spent traveling had accelerated. These large meetings were held monthly, if not bimonthly. Balancing the management of church, family, and travel was becoming a big challenge. Being so busy serving God in so many areas, unfortunately, our children were being neglected. Even though they were always well cared for by our God-given governess, Paula, they desperately needed their parents—us.

We attempted to be obedient to God's call upon our lives and made adjustments as He led us. Obedience always creates a win-win situation for everyone. Certainly God would never ask us to bear children and then put the responsibility of rearing them fully upon someone else. He provided the help that was needed, but ultimately, we as parents were responsible in God's eyes for the nurturing and training of our children.

Psalm 127:3–5 in *The Living Bible* says,

*Children are a gift from God; they are his reward. Children born to a young man are like sharp arrows to defend him. Happy is the man who has his quiver full of them.*

Our quiver was full of four beautiful daughters, each distinctly different in personality: Charity, Spice, Melody, and Abigail.

There were times when we went at such a fast pace in ministry that we starved our four children of adequate attention and family fellowship time. Solomon had much to say about training and disciplining our children in the book of Proverbs. How can we train and discipline them if we are away from them extensively in their early years? How can we make a deposit in them if we aren't around? History will repeat itself if we aren't willing to be sensitive to the Word of

God and to the Spirit of God. In Melody's voice, I recognized the abandonment I felt as a child when my parents were so busy ministering.

As all things with God, seasons change, and our lives were redirected down another path. Our children were entering their teenage years, and they needed us at home. With my parents getting older, the Healing Explosions were less frequent, and life was slowing down. Our traveling was done and the pressure was lessening. We could now concentrate on the children, the church, and ourselves.

However, instead of growing and prospering, the church seemed to be dwindling. Members moved, left, went on to their own ministries. No specific negative reasons were given, but I knew something was happening.

I prayed so hard during that time. I wanted God to show us what we needed to do next to progress to another level with Him in our family and church.

With all the traveling and constant activity around us, my relationship with my husband was slowly but surely changing. I wondered what was going on but assumed that we were just too busy and that things would get back to normal when life became less complicated.

I asked him many times, "Is there anything that could be hindering our walk with God or His blessings?" He always responded, "No, there isn't anything that I know of."

I was aware that he had been molested by an uncle at the age of eight and had been involved in homosexuality. But he had been prayed for and he claimed that he was free—that it would never be part of his life again. Knowing the power of God to set someone free, I trusted him, not realizing it still had a stronghold on him. I believed him when he said, "Everything is fine."

He was under a lot of pressure, traveling and trying to handle all the responsibilities of maintaining a church and family. During this time, a young man assisted him as his traveling companion to handle all the little details while he ministered and met with pastors. This young man was eager to do anything and everything to get his approval. Being a brilliant man, my husband twisted Scripture to influence his assistant. He manipulated the story of Jonathan and David's relationship by telling the young man that Jonathan did anything and everything that David wanted him to do. In the gay community, this list of requests is often misinterpreted to include a homosexual relationship.

I found out about this affair after the fact. I had to deal with serious feelings of betrayal. I confronted him and he confessed it and said that it was a one-time thing. In my willingness to maintain my family and ministry, I chose to believe him. As a Christian, I knew I needed to forgive him because I had made a vow to love, honor, and cherish. So I did, we went to counseling, and he said he was fine again. Now knowing he was *not* fine, we continued on.

We worked hard with church members trying to build a strong base and to reach out to the community. But with every step we took forward, we seemed to fall two steps back. Things were not going well, but there were no obvious answers to the question, "Why?"

To help with the finances, I went to work for a large automotive dealership in the Dallas area. I had never had a secular job in my life and I had no idea if I could survive in that world, let alone make a living. A friend who worked with me assured me I could both survive and succeed. I wasn't so sure. I had spent years talking on the phone for the ministry and quickly found out I could use those same talents for a secular company. After the first few months, I got an award for outstanding achievement (110 percent club). What a surprise! I was worthwhile! I could contribute! I could bring money into the house to help out!

> If we say, "I want to do it my way, God," while God says, "I want you to do it My way," we won't get anywhere.
>
> If we get our life in line with the Word of God, the windows of heaven will open in every area of our life.

But the more I would go and go and try and try, I would just get more black and blue because I was trying to knock those doors down in my own strength. I knew where I needed to go, but I couldn't get through in the natural. I didn't understand what was going on. I had co-pastored a church in Dallas for eighteen years. It had flourished, and then slowly we went into a slump, but instead of recovering, it just continued to spiral downward.

Eventually, we were forced to close the church. For eighteen years, that church was our life and source of income, and suddenly, it was gone. Old feelings of failure poured over me. *I must have done something wrong. What could I do to fix things? Why, God, why?* Rejection, pain, low self-esteem, depression, all came pouring back over me.

We faced financial devastation because we had a house and a car to pay for with no source of adequate income. We started going into debt. We used our credit card to make house payments in order to survive. He was trying; I was trying. We just couldn't bring in enough money to meet our financial needs. I had to borrow money for house payments, food, clothing, and other necessities. We were going backward. I was so sure God was going to pull us out on top again.

I questioned, "What is going on here? I give and I give and I give. I give above and beyond my tithe. What is happening?" I really searched my heart. "God, why is this happening to us and our family? If there is anything in my life that is unpleasing to You, please remove it from my life. I want to be totally sold out for You. I want to be used by You. I want to do all I can do for You." I was getting nowhere.

I mentioned to my husband at that time, "Something is blocking the blessings of God. Whatever it is, we need to deal with it and get rid of it so we can go on with God."

He replied, "I don't know of anything."

For twenty-five years, he had been my husband. He had been my pastor for twenty years. He was the father of my children, the head of the house, and the leader of the home. It was actually his responsibility to figure out why the blessings of God were not coming.

We had met at Oral Roberts University in 1972 and got to know each other while attending a Bible study off campus. We became good friends and when we would pray together for people's needs, they would get healed. We felt led to get married and we did in 1974. We loved each other, and I knew

God could use us as a team. We were anointed and were destined to be traveling around the world ministering together.

Now, in my despair, I prayed, "Whatever is done in darkness, may it be revealed in the light. If there is something in my heart that I have hid that is keeping me from doing what You want me do, please, God, reveal it to me. And if there is something in his life, please reveal it to him and to us so that we can deal with it, get rid of it, and go on with You and do what we are supposed to be doing."

> When you pray for the hidden things to be revealed, you need to be prepared to deal with them.

When you pray like I did, you need to be willing to deal with whatever is revealed. If something is there, I can guarantee you that it is going to come out. If it is there, it will be revealed in the light.

Indeed, it was revealed through a series of circumstances. The fact that my husband had had an affair with another man was hard enough to deal with. Suddenly, it was revealed that not only was he having affairs, he had been having affairs with other men for years.

I had always had my suspicions, whether from phone messages or the way he acted. When I confronted him, he denied it all, of course.

Then, one day, I intercepted a phone call. Somebody wanted to sleep with him and do some other things with him... *again*. My greatest fear was confirmed. He had gone back to, or had been continuing in, an active homosexual lifestyle. At that point, I knew I had had enough. I knew I could not live like that any longer.

I had faithfully prayed for twenty-five years. He had betrayed me as a pastor, as my husband, and as a traveling companion with my parents. When that door of information opened, a lot of other things came with it like a flood.

When there is compromise in one area of your life, there is compromise in many areas. If a person is having affairs or into pornography, he or she is more than likely involved with other things, as well. His actions were brought out into the light, a giant spotlight. When I would ask about these things, he lied every time.

Now, when the truth was undeniable, I fell on my face before God. At that point, I said, "Thus far, and no more. I understand why the blessings of God have stopped in our life the last few years."

Needless to say, an unbelievable, unexpected bomb had gone off in our home that tore our marriage apart.

For years, I had stood by him and believed God for him to remain faithful in the marriage. I couldn't divorce a man on a whiff of suspicion. I had to have concrete proof that he had been unfaithful in the marriage, especially since we were in the ministry. When the call came in from one of his lovers, I started divorce proceedings the next day. Enough with the lies. Enough with the abuse. Enough with the desertion. I had denied the truth of our relationship. Suddenly, I had to face facts.

I knew I didn't have to allow that kind of deception. However, I was so scared. After twenty-five years of marriage, I knew I couldn't survive without him and his financial abilities. He was sure I would never divorce him because he knew what a wimp I was. He knew I would never leave him. He knew I would never give up our home. He had started working in the secular world doing motivational speaking and was very successful. He believed I would never leave the tens of thousands of dollars he was making in the secular world.

He didn't need me for anything, but I had become dependant upon him for everything for so long. He made all the decisions. He was the ultimate leader; I was the follower. Could I really step out from under him and survive? I was so scared, I was overwhelmed with fear—I was petrified.

In a fog of despair, I called a lawyer and started the paperwork. I couldn't believe the dream had dissolved and floated away into nothingness. I couldn't believe that God wanted this to happen.

But I had begged God to reveal the truth, and He had.

The first step is to acknowledge what you have to do. According to Matthew 5:32; 19:9; and other passages, because my husband had an affair, I was free to divorce him. It was hard. He thought I would never leave him, but I could not allow the sin in his life to destroy mine. If you are faced with an impossible situation, know that God will provide a way out for you. He still has a plan for your life.

"God, now what?"

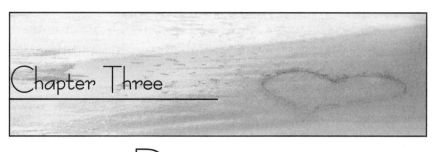

# Chapter Three

# Devastation

nitially, I felt that I had to keep up a front for the children. I didn't want to tell them anything. They probably suspected something was happening, but they never could have imagined something like this!

I asked myself, *Could I break up the family?* But I realized that I wasn't the one who broke it up. He had already ripped it apart. The pieces hadn't fallen quite yet, but I knew I had to put a stop to the sham of our marriage. I took one step and then another and then another. I broke away. It was the hardest thing I have ever had to do.

My mom would call me several times every day and ask, "How are you doing?"

"Horrible, Mom."

And she would call me again later to ask, "How are you doing?"

"Horrible, Mom."

We would hang up and then repeat the same miserable conversation time after time after time amidst my tears. She was trying so hard, but she didn't have an answer. She wasn't the answer.

My whole body felt paralyzed. I could not even make a decision for myself. I would be fine for awhile and then fall into deep despair.

I didn't forget to eat. I couldn't eat. I was so sickened by the whole situation, so much panic, so much fear, so much everything, that there was no way I could put food in my mouth, swallow, and try somehow to keep it down. Over a three-month period, I lost approximately thirty-five pounds. I got to the point that I had to force-feed myself. I knew I was going to die. I knew if I didn't starve myself to death, some other catastrophe was going to take me.

From the depths of my pain, I would look at my girls and think, *They need me.*

Like the woman with the issue of blood (see Matthew 9:20–22), with the little strength that I had, I would take my fork and put the fork into a piece of food. Even though I wanted to throw up, I would put the food in my mouth. As I would chew it, I would tell myself, "This bite is for Charity." I would take another and say, "This bite is for Spice." Then I would take one for Melody and then one for Abigail. And then I would start over again, because I knew four bites of food would not sustain me.

I was in unbelievable, paralyzing pain. But I ate...for my children. When my spirit and heart broke, I wanted to give up. But their love reached out to me, and I had to respond to them. I couldn't give up even though I felt completely devastated.

Ironically, even in the midst of one of the most horrible times in my life, God blessed me with one of the highest honors I've ever received. The automotive dealership where

I had been working for several years presented me with the Extra Mile Award, the highest honor they give.

When I first started working at the company, I knew how to spell the word *computer*, but that was the extent of my knowledge about them. Within a few years, I was overseeing the database of eighteen car dealerships as well as all the printing, the surveys, and the reports related to the used car and body shops. Day after day, I would sit at the computer in my office and cry, enter data, cry, wipe my eyes, and enter data. I fought so hard to make it through every workday.

My coworkers were great. They helped to build up my self-esteem. I finally knew that I could make something of myself outside of his world.

However, my husband wasn't out of my world yet. Before we sold the house, I was living there. While I was at work, he would come back and take various possessions that he wanted to keep. He took more and more and more things. I would often think, *Haven't you taken enough?*

God made a way where there seemed to be no way.

I tried very hard to be strong in front of our four daughters. Obviously, they were his children, also. We would often cry together, "What are we going to do? Why is he doing this?"

A spouse doesn't get alimony in the state of Texas. My take-home pay was $1200 a month. The house payment was $1100 a month. There was no way I could make it. For a short time, he did help me some, but his contribution was not enough for us to survive. The girls were too old for child support. I had to start again with nothing. I didn't get the house, and I didn't get the income; however, I got what mattered—the four girls, the two dogs, and the five fish.

After our beautiful, 4000-square-foot home of eighteen years was sold and divided up, I had a whopping $7500 to start my life over. I didn't know how I was going to get into a house. I praise God that He led my parents to give me enough money for the down payment on a home to keep a roof over my children's heads. That was very important for this mother. I didn't want us living out of our car, especially with the dogs and the fish.

Indeed, God made a way where there seemed to be no way in every area of life. I was able to find a home and we moved into a 2000-square-foot house.

I would do what I could to be around the children and be as happy as I could. At night I would go into my bedroom and shut the door. At the time, we had two royal standard poodles, one black and one white. Chanel, the white one, was his dog. She didn't understand where he went. I felt like she understood what I was feeling. She had been deserted, also. She was the only one who ever heard me cry, the only one who had any clue of what I did behind closed doors. Chanel was a loyal friend. She stood by me through thick and thin. She tried so hard but couldn't stop my pain or hers.

It was a long, hard road. I didn't know where money was going to come from. I sold everything of value that I could, including my wedding ring and other jewelry. Trying to regroup, the girls and I went through many interesting, highly challenging times. Many, many days there was no money for food, and food would appear suddenly from nowhere. Miracle by miracle, the girls and I saw God work on our behalf. When we needed something, we would pray. Before long, our need was taken care of, and we praised God and danced through the house rejoicing.

At first, I felt deserted by my friends. As they found out what was happening to our family, they didn't know what to do. They had absolutely no clue what to say to me or how to deal with me. There was silence as they tried to process and deal with their own feelings of betrayal and grief. They couldn't believe what was happening, either. We had been their pastors, their confidantes. He had been their pastor and their friend. Some people had suspected something was going on with him, but they hadn't said anything. Now, they didn't want to take sides. They had known of situations that had occurred, and felt guilty they hadn't done something, anything, earlier.

No one knew what to say to me to make things better. Most of my friends attended the church. This whole circumstance was as devastating to them as it was to me. They were hurting, too. Often, we would end up in tears together.

A good friend, Paula, was our children's governess while we traveled on the road. Her husband, Mark, said, "I don't know what to say. I can't handle a woman crying around me." He really is a wonderful man and friend, but he didn't know what to do for me.

I said, "Just sit there and listen. Hold my hand. Tell me I will be okay."

There are times you want to be left alone. And there are times when you know it is better for you not to be left alone. I didn't want to be left alone during that time. I was never actually suicidal, although I didn't really have a desire to live. I made sure I was around my Spirit-filled Christian friends who would encourage me.

In Texas, a divorce happens fairly quickly. Within three months after filing, that fateful day arrived. I went to court and cried throughout the divorce proceedings. They kept trying to record the testimony, but I was crying so hard they almost postponed it. My tears prevented me from speaking loud enough to be recordable. The judge gave me his box of tissues. He knew I didn't want the divorce.

Three of my girls were with me, and we all cried the whole time. The last thing in the world I wanted was to be divorced. I don't believe in divorce, but I was forced to deal with the situation and do something I didn't want to do. The gavel went down. I was divorced. At that point, I ran out of the courtroom wailing.

> There is a special bond between fathers and daughters. Girls love their dads in a special way.

Our youngest child was seventeen, so there was no reason to file for child support. I was stuck. He agreed to pay a certain amount of money to me every month, which was a tremendous blessing; however, it was not enough to put the girls through college or provide a home for them.

It was like a bomb went off in our home, scattering us. The security of a united family was destroyed. With the three girls in college and the other working after graduating from college, they went one way, and I went another. We sold our home. He got a car. I got a car. He had a new job and was making a large amount of money every month. The security I had known for twenty-five years evaporated. I was on my own. I had to find a new home and a new church. Numerous other problems arose as far as the children were concerned. Not to mention, I was falling apart.

Again, I stood in the shower with the water pouring down while I cried, "God, You don't have any idea how bad I hurt. I can't make it through this. I can't make it through this. You have no idea how much this heart and this mind and this body hurt." I was forced to endure. I had to go through it. I couldn't stay in that horrible place. I couldn't wallow in it. I knew that, somehow, I had to dust myself off and go forward.

My mother's marriage to Charles Hunter was one of the greatest blessings of my life. The positive influence that he has had on me and my life is indescribable. When I walk into a room, he still lights up like a light bulb because I am his daughter. I know that I know that I know he loves me with an unconditional love. I know that his love has had a very positive effect on every area of my life through the years.

My daughters were daddy's "little girls." He was always so proud of them and encouraged them to be all they could be. Now they were falling apart. Their home was destroyed. They all went through a lot of confusion. Serious things can happen to a girl when that special bond between father and daughter is damaged. I had no idea how to tell them the lurid details. How do you tell your four beautiful daughters that the man they have adored all their lives is gay? I couldn't find the words. I told him he had to explain to the children what had happened to him and why.

What he told them caused even greater confusion in the girls' minds. He blamed me for the entire breakup of our marriage and our home. He tried to convince them that it was my fault that he was homosexual. He said it was *all* my fault. I had destroyed the home. It was my fault that I filed for divorce. I was the one who caused the breakup of the family. I was the one who caused the demise of the finances. He blamed me, the wife God gave him. I don't claim to have been the perfect wife; however, I don't accept responsibility for his actions against the sanctity of our marriage.

He explained that he was normal and the way God had created him. He took them to gay gathering places and introduced them to his lifestyle. He wanted them to accept him the way he was and act like nothing serious had happened, nothing had changed. The truth of their life, of their father, of their parents' relationship, was nonexistent. The honesty of their home life was a sham.

The entire situation was very difficult for the children. For awhile, they did blame me for destroying their home. At that point, I had not only lost my home, I felt like I had lost everything.

The Lord said, "Just be strong, be still. Your children will know the truth someday." It took some time for the girls to realize that their father was not only lying to me, but to them, also. I praise God that He has restored that precious loving relationship between my daughters and me.

When I entered into marriage, I never expected to get a divorce. I planned to grow old with him. Then he told me our marriage was just an act; he had just used me. I gave him twenty-five years of my life, and I was still in love with the man when the gavel went down.

Because friends had no idea what to do or say, they avoided me. The feelings of rejection bounced all around me. I felt abandoned again. All I wanted from them was to hear they still loved me and that they would stand with me and pray for me. I did what I could do to be around my friends. I was unashamed about what I was going through even though I felt as if I had a big red "D" for *divorced* on a chain wrapped around my neck. I was ostracized by many people, because you just don't get divorced in the church, especially when you are in the ministry. I gravitated to my friends who were very close to me. I desperately needed friends who would stick closer than a brother. I knew I couldn't make it on my own.

> Sometimes friends don't understand. I needed a friend who would stick closer than a brother.

Some friends and a few family members remarked, "Thank God, you aren't married to him anymore." I knew they meant well and were trying to help; but the truth was, I didn't want to be divorced. I was glad I wasn't married to him anymore if he was going to continue in the same behavior, but I just couldn't get over this kind of trauma quickly. I just couldn't wake up the next morning and say, "I'm *so* glad I'm divorced after twenty-five years of marriage."

Morning after morning, when I opened my eyes, I had to remind myself that my world was totally different. I was in a different house. I didn't have a husband to help take care of me anymore. I had to use every inch of my faith for food, housing, utilities, gas, and the girls every single minute of every single day of every single week, with no end in sight.

I was not only dealing with my pain, I was dealing with the pain of all my friends from the loss of their pastor, the pain of my children from the loss of their father—and he was their pastor, too. You can imagine the impression the girls and my friends had of God, pastors, fathers, and church. When something this traumatic happens, most people are tempted to seclude themselves, separate themselves from others to re-group and lick their wounds. There was a time that I felt that way, too; however, I knew I had to get out of the house even though I didn't want to. I didn't want to be seen because of the embarrassment of the divorce, but I pushed myself.

Going to church for the first time after the divorce felt so strange. Because we were well known in the Dallas area, I felt that everyone was judging me. I was going to church to hear His Word of refreshing, to be loved on, and enjoy His presence. I really didn't want anyone's pity or looks of disapproval. I needed His total peace. To feed my devastated and starved spirit, I went to as many church services as I could, listened to teaching tapes, and desperately hung on to His promises.

I was still working at the automotive dealership at the time. It took me so long to accomplish anything. I thank God for a manager who understood what was going on and patiently worked with me during that time to get me through. I had worked above and beyond the call of duty for many years at that office.

They knew I would make it through this situation because I had been a very reliable employee for all those years. But it was so hard to keep my mind on work. Thoughts of the girls would pour over me. How would I pay for their needs? What if they got sick or had an accident? They are all smart and need to continue their education. How would I pay for tuition? And then the rejection, pain, and tears would come again.

My relationship with God never wavered. One day I was having a very hard time at the office and I felt so alone. I had written an e-mail to a friend, "I am going through so much stuff between me, the girls, finances, and everything else. I feel so alone."

She wrote me back and said, "I just pray right now that God will walk in and put His arms around you and tell you how much He loves you."

Before I actually got the message, I felt a presence enter my office and put comforting arms around me. I knew it was the presence of God, the Holy Spirit, and Jesus. I knew He was there with me. As I read the e-mail, I looked around to see who was touching me, who had a hand on my shoulder. When I got the e-mail from her, I knew there was power in her prayers. I thank God for what a good friend she was during this time. She had experienced a similar situation and was able to help me from a standpoint of someone who had been there, done that, and had successfully survived an equally horrible situation.

I knew I had a choice to make. What was I going to do with this situation? Was I going to be bitter, or was I going to get better? Was I going to dig a hole and get into it and stay there forever? Or was I going to get mad at the devil? I knew where the attack was coming from; however, getting up the energy to fight and stand against him was so hard.

I was climbing the steepest mountain I had ever encountered. I knew God was at the peak of that mountain, but I was a million miles below inside a dark pit. I surrounded myself with beautiful praise music and teaching tapes. When my pain and crying overpowered the music, I would turn up the volume until it drowned out my noisy sobbing.

I had to take a stand. I said, "I refuse to let the enemy keep me a crying and blubbering faucet." I was a wreck. I called out to God. I screamed out to Him. I wanted to wallow in my pain and self-pity. I didn't want to bother other people but I knew deep inside that I couldn't forsake the fellowship of other Christians.

> God will never leave you or forsake you.

In order to get through this, I had to depend on God more than ever before because I felt more alone than ever before. I played praise and worship CDs constantly in my car, at work, and at home. The only peace I found was while I was lost in worshipping God, knowing He was the only One who would get me through this time in my life, who would never abandon or desert me. He was the only constant in my life. He would always be with me and love me.

Even though the divorce was final, the battles didn't stop. But the battles were no longer just between the two of us. Now, the battle was also within me. All my old fears flooded my mind. The spirit of desertion had found a foothold. My biological father had abandoned me as a child. My husband had deserted me. My children were essentially gone. One by one, they drifted away, out on their own to find their own answers, to live their own lives. They didn't need Mom much. The nest was empty. Every time I said good-bye to someone, I had the fear that I would never see him or her again.

I was married at twenty years of age, remained married for twenty-five years, and endured a lot of unlovely times as well as unloved times. I had been faithful to my husband beyond words. I supported him even though he didn't always deserve to be supported—but that's the job of a wife. I was always there for him. I was always there for the girls. I tried to be there for all the church members. Why wasn't someone there for me now? I felt so alone.

We had been in ministry. We had traveled the world helping at most of the Healing Explosions, the majority of which he had orchestrated. Yet there was something missing in our marriage, and I didn't understand what it was. Now, I was informed that it was all me. That I was ugly. I was fat. I was stupid. I was like his sister rather than his wife. We had a very good relationship on a superficial level. We were very good friends, but the intimacy in the relationship was not there. I didn't understand why. I had nothing to compare our marriage to. I could not satisfy him in many areas because I wasn't what he wanted. He wasn't satisfied with who he was, so nothing I could do was satisfying to him, either.

I knew there wasn't any way I could survive and make it through. Night after night, I would cry, "God, You don't have any idea how bad I hurt. I can't make it through this. I can't make it through this. You haven't any idea how much this heart, this mind, and this body hurt."

One night, in His beautiful still small voice, I heard God say, "You think I don't know? Yes, I do. I had to turn My back on My own Son on the cross for you so that you wouldn't have to bear this pain. I know what pain is. I know the pain you are feeling."

I quickly apologized to God. "Father, forgive me. You *do* understand the pain I am going through, but only You can take the pain away."

No, there weren't any lightning flashes. The pain wasn't miraculously gone. I still had to walk through more trials. At this point, I felt my life was threatened. I didn't want to put my life as a woman or as a mother at risk. He had not been with another woman; he had been intimate with other men. When our marriage covenant had been broken, he had also opened the door to diseases.

I had to accept that I could possibly have AIDS or be HIV positive. I had to go to the laboratory month after month, saying, "Take my blood again. Take my blood again."

And every time I would claim, "God, I thank You that I'm not going to be HIV positive. I can eat any deadly thing. I can be around any deadly disease and it shall not harm me. I stand on Your promise." (See Mark 16:18.)

But they still had to take my blood and I still had to wait two weeks to get the results. I was negative for the disease. A few months would go by and they would take my blood again. For two years, I had to endure the procedure every few months and wait for the results. Praise God, I was clear. But it was two years of hell to go through that procedure time after time.

Thank You, God. You are so faithful.

Two days after the divorce was final, I had my annual mammogram. The doctor gave me the report: "It shows cancer this time."

Only two days after my divorce!

God, haven't I had enough? My marriage
is dead. Do I have to die, too?

I will discuss my battle with breast cancer in chapter six. Sometimes, when one thing goes wrong, it seems like the floodgates open and suddenly everything in our world is falling apart. We think, *Job has nothing on me! This is real pain.* Our friends can't help us because they don't have the answers, no matter how hard they try to be supportive. At these times, it's important to get alone with God. Yell at Him if you need to. Tell Him exactly what you are feeling. He can handle it. And then be sure to listen for His response. He's there, He cares, and He'll make a way when there seems to be no way.

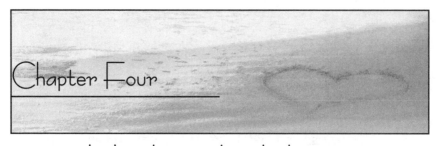

# Chapter Four

# Healing the Heart

Several years ago, Charity, my oldest daughter, was having trouble accepting the fact that she is beautiful. I told her quite emphatically that she is beautiful. Of course, her response was, "You're supposed to say that; you're my mom."

I prayed for God to show her that she is indeed beautiful, not only in God's eyes, but in others' eyes, also. Later that week, I took her to a Margaret Becker concert. Margaret was her favorite recording artist at the time. At the end of the concert, Charity wanted to get Margaret's autograph so she was the first in line to talk to her. As Margaret was handing the paper with the autograph back to Charity, she looked at Charity and said, "You are beautiful. You are a very beautiful young lady."

Thank you, Margaret Becker; but most of all, thank You, Jesus! It was just what Charity needed to hear and from the person she needed to hear say it.

Too many of us are sitting on our potential. I sat on mine for many years! I knew God had anointed me and given me many abilities. I knew I wanted to teach and travel, but instead, I hid. I appreciate what my mom and dad have done in my life to make me do things I didn't want to do at the time.

Has a parent or someone else you love ever made you do things that you really didn't want to do? You were angry at the time, but grew to love them later for their persistence. Then, you made your own children do the same thing! That's my story!

First Chronicles 16:11 says, "*Seek the LORD and His strength; seek His face continually*" (NASB). If we sought God's face every day, we wouldn't be just "pew potatoes"—those who go to church and listen to the message but are just about as affected by it as something they watch on TV. We wouldn't be able to contain all that God would show us. We are to seek His face continually. Not once a day or once a week, but continually. God wants to spend that time with us.

> If ye continue in my word, then are ye my disciples indeed; and ye shall know the truth, and the truth shall make you free.
> —John 8:31–32 KJV

I thank God for my healing. How often? I didn't just pray and quit. I didn't pray for God to heal my personality and get my mind all straightened out and then forget about it. I thank Him continually, especially for the changes still being made.

The truth will set us free. That's great, but how do we know the truth? If we continue in His Word, then we will know the truth and the truth will set us free! His truth set me free!

Faith comes by hearing and hearing by the Word of God. As we hear the Word of God again and again, our faith grows. Jesus is saying, "Continue in My Word and the truth will make you free." (See John 8:31–32.)

This passage of Scripture doesn't say, "Read My Word when you feel like it." It says, "Continue in My Word." Does it say that you have arrived when you read it the first time? No. When you pray the first time for your healing, whether it is physical, emotional, or spiritual, does it say pray once and stop? No. It says, "Continue in My Word." Why? So we can continually be strengthened spiritually, emotionally, and physically.

We need to improve ourselves every day in our manners, our speech, our makeup, and our appearance. We need to look like we are our Father's children. We need to look like the One whom we serve. If I still weighed almost 280 pounds, didn't have any makeup on, and didn't have my hair washed or fixed, you wouldn't care to listen to me, and I wouldn't blame you. But, when you look nice and smell nice, people will want to listen to you, they will want to be around you, and they will want to hear whatever you have to say.

The truth of His Word will liberate you.

I praise God that I have been set free. During the majority of my life, I lived in bondage with a shell around me keeping me from doing what God wanted me to do. That shell was melted by Jesus Christ as I allowed the power of God to flow through me in a mighty way.

Does Psalm 34:1 say, "His praises shall come out of my mouth on Sunday?" No! It says, *"I will bless the LORD at all times; His praise shall continually be in my mouth."*

Our praises are a fragrance to the Lord, and He likes breathing that sweet aroma. Should we praise Him for our healing once? No. If we show our earthly father appreciation continually when he does something for us, he will want to do things for us again. If we continually praise our heavenly Father, we draw closer to Him and become more complete physically, emotionally, and spiritually.

He says, "Don't look through your eyes; look through Mine."

You may be thinking, "I am not a fighter." You need to be. If someone steals something from you, don't you want to get that property back? If the devil has taken something from you, don't you want to get it back? He has trespassed on your territory where he doesn't belong. His job is to steal, kill, and destroy. (See John 10:10.) He chips away at all of us mentally, emotionally, and spiritually. He steals peace, kills spirit, and destroys confidence as well as many other aspects of life. If he has convinced you that you are a failure and that you will never amount to anything, prove him wrong. I have.

God is Love.

My teachers told me I would never accomplish anything and that the only thing I would be able to do is wash dishes. I have washed a lot of dishes for my family and the many guests I have entertained at home. However, I have never washed dishes for a living and I don't intend to because of the power of God in my life and the calling of God upon my life.

There is a powerful, miraculous God who wants to set you free. You have been wasting your potential and using all of the excuses the enemy has given you. If you get rid of those excuses, he will come up with more. I can testify to that. I frequently came up with a whole new list of excuses! But, the God who took care of the first list can take care of the second list and the third and the fourth and any after that.

If God were to be described in one word, what would it be?

LOVE!

Yes, He's wonderful. Yes, He's awesome. Yes, He's El Shaddai. Yes, He's our provider. He is everything. But all that He is can be encapsulated in the word *love*.

> A merry heart does good, like medicine, but a broken spirit dries the bones.
> —Proverbs 17:22

Do you love from your brain? Do you love from your elbow?

No, you love from your heart.

If you cannot love God, you cannot love your neighbor, and you cannot love yourself. And the reason you cannot love is that your heart is hurting.

Why do you think the enemy is doing everything he can do to destroy people's hearts? He's going for the jugular vein of Christianity. He's not messing with a little finger. He's going for the heart.

I believe that is one of the main reasons why God is raising me up right now. Number one, we are seeing the expression of God's love in sending His Son in a greater way. But, you have to let go of the hurts of the past.

A broken heart, a broken spirit, can literally make you physically sick. The word *heart* is used in the Bible 948 times.

The word *love* is used 620 times. Obviously, this has great importance and needs to be dealt with on a regular basis.

So much of what I have been through was certainly not from heaven; it was straight from the pit of hell. But I survived. Today, I can tell you that no matter what you have been through or are going through, you can survive, too.

Experts say there are ten traumatic events that could ruin your life or even cause enough stress to literally kill you, such as a move from city to city, or house to house, illness, or divorce, just to name a few. Such stress can have a seriously destructive effect on any person. Any one of the ten can be absolutely devastating beyond words. I had nine of the stressors in one year. And I'm here to tell about it. I'm here to tell you how God completely saved me and brought me out of it, so that I'm now standing on solid ground. I'm here as a testimony because, yes, I passed the test.

I had some photos taken. No, not a glamour shot. I was simply sitting in front of a camera smiling. They turned out great! Even I was amazed. When I showed my brother, he said, "Who is that?" Actually, he gasped for breath because he couldn't believe the photo was of his kid sister. I gave one to my parents for Christmas in a nice crystal frame. They both started weeping. It wasn't bad. It was a good weep. They wept over what God had done for me.

But the important photo I want to describe is many years old. There is absolutely no similarity between the recent photo and the older one. Yes, I know it is me, but I can't even relate to who the person was. The drastic change in my life shows in my pictures. It shows in my face. It shows in my eyes.

A lady saw me one recent Valentine's Day. We hadn't seen each other in ten or fifteen years. She called me the next day to say, "You are beautiful. You have turned into a beautiful lady."

I said, "Thank you, thank you, thank you." She repeated her compliment several times and then she called my mother to tell her what a beautiful daughter she had.

The old photo shows how much I was hurting. I didn't understand why I was in that particular situation. I felt very, very unloved and extremely unlovely. The difference in my weight between the two photographs is approximately one hundred pounds. Yes, I lost weight, I cut my hair, I got Lasik done, but those cosmetic changes weren't what made the biggest difference. I have a whole new attitude and confidence.

> God is making me into who I was destined to be.

I am writing now from a healed heart. And I have such a burning desire, an unbelievable, almost uncontrollable compassion, to reach in and do whatever I can do to help heal other people's hearts just like He has done for me. God is making me into who I was destined to be.

I got saved when I was twelve years old and never backslid. Don't plan on ever backsliding. I have hit a few potholes, but you know what? I just dusted myself off and kept on going.

There is a guest coordinator for a local Houston television station who is also a wonderful lady. She called me up one Sunday morning after seeing me from a distance at church the night before. "What has happened to you? You look totally different."

I hadn't seen her in six months, but you would have thought it had been six years! I said, "I'm happier than I have ever been in my life. I am set free from the guilt and the shame from the past. The past belongs to somebody else."

The past doesn't belong to the present me. Yes, I can remember the story. I can tell the story the same way because I have a good memory. But it isn't mine anymore. I chose to release it.

God has done marvelous things. Not only is the natural man not recognizable, so is the spirit man. Everything about me has changed. God gets all the glory!

Proverbs 15:13 says, *"A merry heart makes a cheerful countenance, but by sorrow of the heart the spirit is broken."*

God understood my pain. He understands your pain, as well.

Psalm 56:8 says,

*You have seen me tossing and turning through the night. You have collected all my tears and preserved them in your bottle! You have recorded every one in your book.* (TLB)

Why does He record every one of our tears? There are many interpretations of this passage, but I will give you mine. *Restoration.*

I am claiming a hundredfold return on every tear I have shed and every heartache I have endured. He has recorded every hurt. He has truly replaced every ache, every pain, and

He has given me joy in the morning and beauty for ashes. (See Isaiah 61:3.) Do you know the symbolism of ashes in the Jewish tradition? When somebody dies, the mourners wear ashes on their foreheads for seven to thirty days, depending on which tradition they follow. At the end of the period, they simply say, "It is time to get over it."

We are given a period of time to get over things and then we must get on with our lives. Ecclesiastes 3:4 talks about a time to weep, a time to laugh, a time to mourn, and a time to dance. It's only a period of time and then we need to get over it.

> God whispered in my spirit, "I have it all worked out. You just need to walk it out."

Recently, a lady came up to me in a service and said, "I lost my husband to a younger woman."

She was very sad, and I don't want to make light of this because she was really hurting.

I asked, "How long has it been?"

She said, "Twenty years."

I looked at her and said, "It is time to get over it. He's gone. He's not coming back. Do you realize you have allowed the enemy to steal twenty years of your life, your joy, your everything because of the pain?"

But you know what? It is much easier said than done.

I remember God saying to me through His Holy Spirit, "I have it all worked out. You just have to walk it out." He was right. He had it all worked out. I had to walk it out by faith one day at a time.

I had to forgive. I had to give my hurts to the Lord.

You need to know that your steps are ordered by the Lord. (See Psalm 37:23.) God has called you and will raise you up like a phoenix. Even though, in the natural, there is no way that you can recover after death, you are going to rise up mightier than ever before. I have risen like a mighty eagle to fly high above the storms of life. And these wings are getting stronger and stronger and stronger. I am soaring to where God wants me to go. You can, too!

The enemy has done everything he can do to snuff my fire out. He poured water on it. He poured negative words into my mind. He poured bad situations around me. He poured desertion on me. The attacks didn't come from just one person. The negative comments came from every direction. Just as I thought things might be getting better, I would receive more and more from somewhere else.

The old saying is, "Sticks and stones may break my bones, but words will never hurt me." But it is wrong! Not true!

My version would read: "Sticks and stones may break my bones, but words hurt even more."

Most people don't realize the truth of my version. If you are going through the effects of a situation in your life, whether it occurred twenty days or twenty years ago, God wants you free. He wants you *free.*

As I shared before, I often couldn't see the computer screen to do my work because tears were pouring out of my eyes. When you are hurting so much, you cannot see clearly. At that point, you need to call on God more than you have ever called on Him in your life. You need a clearer vision than you have ever experienced in your life.

The tears will dry up. God will heal your heart. But you must be willing. When you are dealing with a broken heart, depressed and crying, you will get a lot of attention. Some people are willing to sacrifice their joy in the Lord for the negative attention that people will give them. I would rather get attention from laying hands on the sick and seeing them recover. I want to lay hands on the brokenhearted and see them set free. I would rather get attention from the miraculous acts that the Lord is performing through me, so I can draw the attention to Him and what He has done. It is up to you to make that choice.

> Keep your heart with all diligence, for out of it spring the issues of life.
> —Proverbs 4:23

"*The* LORD *is near to those who have a broken heart*" (Psalm 34:18). And do you know why He is there? Because He has a heart of compassion. His heart has been broken. How many times have we broken His heart? Not just when He was on the cross. He loves us unconditionally, but it still hurts Him when we do something in disobedience or don't do something out of a lack of obedience.

*Create in me a clean heart, O God, and renew a steadfast spirit within me.* (Psalm 51:10)

You can't expect God to heal a heart that is full of unforgiveness. If you read all of Psalm 51, you will find it is a chapter on unforgiveness. You need to repent of unforgiveness, not just obvious sins you have committed. Get rid of sin. Get rid of unforgiveness. Get rid of stinking thinking and bad attitudes. He wants a clean heart.

The most important thing we can do is adjust our attitudes. We must be washed in the water of the Word. (See Ephesians 5:26.) As we come to see ourselves as God sees us, through the blood of Jesus—delivered, whole, set free, accomplishing great things for the kingdom—the negative words others have spoken over us won't have as much power. We can rebuke those negative attacks. When Peter said, in effect, "God forbid that You should die, Jesus," Jesus responded, *"Get behind Me, Satan."* (See Matthew 16:22–23.) He knew the Father's plan and He wouldn't allow negative words to deter Him. He recognized that the words weren't coming from His friend Peter but from Satan. Our enemy is subtle and we must learn to recognize his attacks and combat him with the Word.

# Chapter Five

# Walking Out Your Healing

I f you talk to someone who is hurting, you will hear what the person is feeling as they speak.

"How are you?"

"Fine." In that monotone voice, they tell you they are *not* fine.

You can say, "Great," and walk away, or you can say, "No, really, how are you?"

I walked into the doctor's office one day for my annual checkup. She came in and said, "How are you?"

I said quietly, "Fine."

She said, "No, how are you? How are you handling being alone? How are you?"

I said, "I'm really great. Traveling all over the world. Seeing people healed and set free."

She said, "Wow! That's great. What makes the difference is your attitude."

Am I ever lonely? *Yes.* I'm human. It is not good for man or woman to be alone. Traveling can be especially lonely.

*Anxiety in the heart of man causes depression, but a good word makes it glad.* (Proverbs 12:25)

Positive words of affirmation make people feel good and want to do even better. If all a person hears is negative words, he or she is crushed and afraid to try again.

During a meeting at the house one night, I asked the people to critique my ideas for a meeting to be held the coming weekend. However, I also explained I didn't want to be crucified. Jesus experienced the cross and that was enough. One of my love languages is affirmation. Cheer me on and I will try to do better and better. Tearing me apart can shut me down.

Anxiety of the heart just causes depression. What happens when someone believes in you? What happens when someone gives you an encouraging word? Your spirit soars. You want to do more, be more, love more.

...the eyes of your understanding being enlightened; that you may know what is the hope of His calling.
—Ephesians 1:18

While growing up, we all heard our mothers or fathers say, "If you can't say anything nice, don't say anything at all." If you can't say anything nice to someone, especially one who is hurting, don't say anything. Just be there.

The worst thing you can say is, "Aren't you glad you are divorced?" Marriage is not supposed to end in divorce. Sometimes there is no choice. Sometimes you fall in the ditch and sometimes someone pushes you. I just happened to be pushed. But I got out.

One of my platform Scriptures is found in Ephesians:

*That the God of our Lord Jesus Christ, the Father of glory, may give to you the spirit of wisdom and revelation in the knowledge of Him, the eyes of your understanding being enlightened; that you may know what is the hope of His calling, what are the riches of the glory of His inheritance in the saints, and what is the exceeding greatness of His power toward us who believe, according to the working of His mighty power.* (Ephesians 1:17–19)

When I went to pick up some copies of recent photographs, the photographer said, "I want you to read this magazine. I think this will pertain to what you minister on." He handed me a *National Geographic* magazine. The article was talking about the billions of dollars people have spent to look younger from having their face acid peeled or ripped off, liposuction here, Botox there, eyebrow lift here, and a little nip and tuck there. Literally billions of dollars are spent every year for these procedures. Then there are all the beauty products. Whatever doesn't look younger, you can cover up. Fake it, until you can make it under the knife.

The article talked about the billions and billions of dollars spent when, in reality, the number one thing that will make you look younger is simply touch. Just touch.

My daughter, Melody, often gives me a massage during our visits. I always say, "Please don't stop." Just the touch of another person feels so good. There is just not enough touching. We were created for relationship. We flourish with those relationships. We thrive being touched and loved.

While I was reading, I said, "God, people tell me that I look ten years younger than I did last year or three years ago. I'm getting younger as the days get longer. God, this article says the number one thing that makes you look younger is touch. If anything, that's not what I have had."

In His quiet loving voice, He said, "You have been touched by the Master's hand."

It feels so good to get a massage from someone who loves me as much as my daughter loves me. But all it takes is a touch from the Master's hand.

God showed me that there would be people reading this book, male and female, who were molested as children, who have participated in an abortion, or who have lost a child to abortion. There's a lot of guilt and pain. There have been other abuses—verbal, physical, emotional, sexual. There is simply not enough love, not enough acceptance, not enough touch.

> In His quiet, loving voice, He said, "You have been touched by the Master's hand."

After the touch from the Master's hand, I have no scars, no marks of abuse. There's no scarring present anymore. After I had been so badly abused, neglected, emotionally scarred, did I want to get married again? Yes, because I have so much love to give. In addition to that, there is the need we all have to be loved and to be held.

The hardest thing for me to do on the road is to go back to an empty hotel room and have no one to share things with. Of course, friends are around and I can call them round the clock. But in the privacy of my own room, God has already seen everything that has happened.

I often lie in bed with my arms up, saying, "God, thank You. Thank You for using me. Did you see that guy that the doctors told that he was better off dead? He is now whole and healed. That was really great, God, how You healed that man and You healed that lady of fibromyalgia, too. She couldn't even touch her skin to put on her makeup. And You healed her. Now she is singing and excited because she can do housework again. God, did You see the one who had part of the bone in her arm missing and it grew out?"

God is there with me. And He doesn't say He's tired tonight. He doesn't turn over and go to sleep. I can keep talking all night long. When you go home under the anointing, the last thing you want to do is go to sleep.

Remember these Scriptures:

*Yea, though I walk through the valley of the shadow of death,...thou art with me.* (Psalm 23:4 KJV)

*You intended to harm me, but God intended it for good to accomplish what is now being done, the saving of many lives.* (Genesis 50:20 NIV)

God is taking what has happened in my life and is turning it around to minister to many, many people. He can do the same thing for you. When you walk through a valley, what do you see? A mountain, a stream, trees. God showed me I needed to walk through the valley of the shadow of death with blinders on to the things of the world, the things that surround me. You need to do the same thing. You will be concentrating so hard on getting through the valley that you won't allow other circumstances that come your way to hinder you.

God wants an intimate relationship with you just like He wants with me. That special relationship will change you. It changed me. There is no comparison between the "old" Joan and the "new" Joan. I have been saved since I was twelve years old and my relationship with the Lord was strong. But it was nothing compared to what it is today after walking through the valley of the shadow of death with Him. The attacks were sent to kill me. Instead, they made me stronger.

We all have choices. Bad situations will come our way; the fiery darts are going to attack us. We must put on the shield of protection with many coats of the Word of God to keep those darts from penetrating our hearts.

> Bad situations will come your way. You must put on the shield of protection to keep the darts from penetrating.

Many don't have that close, personal relationship with God. Situations in your life threaten to destroy you or your close family and friends. You may have seen friends who have been attacked lying by the side of the road. Some of them don't even go to church anymore. We have the choice of going *through* the valley of the shadow of death. We have the choice of going *into* the valley and keeling over. We also have the choice of helping each other to our feet and walking through *together*.

How do you get from the valley to the mountaintop? Everybody loves the mountaintop, but what happens on the mountaintop? Have you ever been to the mountaintop? How many people actually stay on the mountaintop? Not many.

How do you get there? No magic carpet rides. You climb one step at a time, one day at a time, one verse at a time, one situation at a time. On your way up, it is not easy. It is not fun. The enemy tries to hit you every which way. He will do whatever he can do to stop you. So you start climbing one step at a time. As you get higher, suddenly, your foot may slip. God has His safety belt around you to protect you from injury. Hang on. Talk to Him. The enemy hates to hear anointed music, so praise Him with a song. Let His Word flow from your mouth as He gives you a song from your heart.

The safety belt of righteousness catches you as you fall. Pick yourself up; put a little spiritual antiseptic healing prayer on your skinned knee. Dust yourself off. Put on your spiritual armor and keep on going. There will be flying rocks trying to knock you down and destroy you. You have to keep going.

## What Do You Do in the Valley?

There are ten things that I have found that will help you make it out of the valley to the mountaintop.

### #1 Communicate with God.

God knows your voice. He hears your cry. He will answer you. Immediately? Maybe. Sometimes, He answers and you don't want to hear it so you just keep asking. He may answer, "Wait. Keep trusting Me." Talk to Him continuously.

He is always there. You don't have to look for Him. You don't have to drive across town to find Him. He hears every word you speak or even think. He knows you better than anyone else in the whole world and loves you unconditionally. Talk to Him. He is your best friend and confidante. He knows and feels everything you do. He is the ultimate answer to absolutely everything.

# #2 Read His Word.

Renew your mind daily with the Word of God. (See Romans 12:2.) In this way, Christ's thoughts will begin to replace negative thoughts. Listen to teaching tapes. Play them at home as you do your daily chores or get ready for work. Play them in the car as you drive. Play them at night as you relax for sleep. Be creative. If you understand best when you read something, read. If you do better by hearing, then listen to all the teaching tapes you can find. If you need to hear yourself speak the Word, then read aloud to yourself. Fill yourself up with the Word because that's the only way you are going to make it.

# #3 Listen to Praise and Worship Music.

Music is so important. It will keep your spirit in tune with God. The anointing flows over you and cuts the problems of the world out of your consciousness. He speaks during these times, also. He is God, He is our Father, He is above every other name, and He is worthy of all our attention and worship. Anointed worship music will give you an idea of what the mountaintop is like and encourages you to keep taking one step at a time.

There were times I couldn't speak, times I didn't know what to pray, or times when I didn't have the energy to move at all. What I could do was repeat the words from a favorite song, the song God would put into my mind for that day.

I told a friend of mine that there needed to be a warning label on her music CDs saying, "Please do not play this at work. You will not get anything accomplished. You will want to stop everything and just worship the Lord."

> There have been two sets of footprints wherever I have walked, one bigger than mine. One that I will never fill, but will never, ever do without.

Many times that year, I asked, "God, where are You?" I played my friend's CD time after time and worshipped the Lord. With tears streaming down my face, I so often repeated, "God, I don't know how I am going to make it." Suddenly, I would feel somebody walk up and put his arms around me. I would turn around to find nobody there.

But He was. God inhabits the praises of His people. No one will ever convince me that it wasn't God, through the Holy Spirit, who came in and put His hand on my shoulder and once again reminded me that I was not alone. He was there. He was directing my every step. He still is, and He is directing yours, also. Yea, though I walk through the valley of the shadow of death, I will fear no evil because my God has walked through it with me. (See Psalm 23:4.) There have been two sets of footprints wherever I have walked, one bigger than mine—one that I will never fill, but will never,

ever do without. Sometimes there was only one set of footprints when He carried me through the really hard times. I knew that I was never alone.

# #4 Repent.

Ask God to forgive you for your part in the problems you are facing. Ask and He will show you where you might have missed His leading and gone your own way. Ask Him for guidance as to what you should do next.

# #5 Forgive.

If you have been the recipient of any type of abuse, ask God to forgive those who have hurt you. Forgive them yourself. Release them from what they did, and ask God to bless them.

Say out loud,

"Father, what (insert the person's name) did to me was sin. It hurt me a lot. It still hurts today. Separate that sin from him/her and put it on the cross. And on the day of judgment, I will hold no accusation against him/her. Father, bless him/her, in Jesus' name."

# #6 Be Selective with Your Environment.

Surround yourself with committed, Spirit-filled Christians who will support you, love you, pray with you, and affirm you. Listen to positive words germinated from His Word. Philosophies of the world can't cut it. Only God's Word and His loving children can help hold you up until you can walk again. It is very important to be among believers. Find somebody in whom you can confide. This may be your pastor or a close Christian friend. You need to feel free to call people and say, "This is an area where I am really weak. I need help." Let them pray with you.

I have a wonderful friend named Catheryne whom I call for support. We cry and pray and weep together. Then I call her back with the victory reports. Don't just weep on their shoulders. Allow them to rejoice with you, also. They are walking through the valley of the shadow of death with you. They are praying you through. We need to stand side by side and help each other through the battles.

> In your trials, fellowship with other believers who will pray with you and cry with you is important.

Fellowship is very important. The Bible instructs us to fellowship one with another. *"Not forsaking the assembling of ourselves together"* (Hebrews 10:25).

People at work would feel sorry for me and say, "Let's go out. Let's go drinking."

I said, "Thanks, but no thanks!" That wasn't the fellowship I was talking about.

Others would speak out in false sympathy, "You will never survive that situation you are going through!"

You may need to confront those people and tell them not to speak those words into your life. If they persist, you may need to avoid them, even if they are related to you. Especially if they are related to you and saying things like, "I just don't know how you are going to make it through this! I don't know what you are going to do!"

I would confidently say, "Well, God bless you all. I'll talk to you later." I'm telling you the truth. I have been there and done that. Sometimes those words have come from friends, sometimes from relatives.

Protect yourself from the negative, and encourage the positive. I was starved. I needed the good food, not the bad.

Just as you need prayers, someone to talk to, and friends around to support you, you also need someone who will hug you. Only you can identify that trusted person or persons who can put their arms around you and hold you and love you and let you cry on their shoulders.*

# #7 Feed Your Spirit.

Attend church services, seminars, conventions, and healing schools. Bask in the glory of His presence, His people, and His Word as it goes forth through anointed men and women of God as they praise and teach. Go as often as you can. Every time the church doors are open, you have the opportunity to be fed and ministered to. If you want God to be there for you in every circumstance, then you need to be willing to support your church, your pastor, and your spiritual leaders. Ask for prayer as often as you feel led. There is such power in agreement. Agree with what you hear them say as they talk to God on your behalf. If you can, get it on tape and listen to it again and again. Tape any words of wisdom or prophecy spoken over you. Listen again and again.

---

* In a vulnerable emotional state, be careful who you accept comfort from and avoid men with less-than-honorable intentions.

Television is available 24/7 with so many choices of anointed teachers to access. Even the Internet opens up thousands of opportunities to learn what others have done to survive the battles. Internet prayers are just as anointed as those given in person. You can print them and read them just as often as you need encouragement. Feed your spirit!

# #8 Seek Professional Help.

If you are going through a very serious situation, you may want to consider a professional Christian counselor. I know some people look down on that choice. A lady called me one day to say, "I went to my pastor and he said that they couldn't help me and that I needed psychotherapy or something. No one understands but you."

God can minister through professionals as well as church leaders. The enemy is attacking in so many areas right now that the average church is not always adequately trained to handle some situations. Members of the local body of Christ are available to pray with you, agree with you, help you, and counsel you in any way they can. However, if you need more, it is not a sin to get the help you need. Find someone to help you. It is important that you find a godly counselor who diagnoses using God's Word first and psychological theories second. If the advice of the counselors does not line up with God's Word, find another person to talk to. If your pastor does not counsel, he may be able to refer you to someone who does.

Professional, Spirit-filled counselors and pastors can often identify problem areas that are obvious to them but often hidden to those buried in pain during a crisis. Glean from their knowledge and wisdom. Then agree in prayer and go to God for His wisdom and your healing.

# #9 Watch Your Words.

Watch what you say and what others say around you. You will see a major turnaround in your life when you edit the comments that are spoken about you. Listen to yourself. Get a tape recorder. What are you saying to your friends? What are you saying at work? What you say can block the blessings of God. I don't want any blessings of God withheld from me. I want all of my blessings. I want you to have yours, too. It is up to you to get yours. It is up to me to get mine.

Hang on. Don't stop. Don't give up! Make a decision to encourage others. Lift their spirits with positive words.

During a teaching at church one Sunday morning, the Holy Spirit spoke to me, "Look at your fingernails." I had painted my nails a bright shade of red. All but one of my nails were long. One fingernail on my right hand had broken off, almost to the quick. I held my hands up before the congregation and asked, "What do you see?" I responded for them, "Some of you see pretty nails. Some of you see bright red fingernail polish. Some of you see pretty hands. Some of you see only the one broken fingernail."

Often, we are so quick to point out the one fault of another person rather than emphasizing the nine positive points. We need to dwell on the positives knowing that the one broken fingernail will grow again.

During one plane flight, I was sharing my story with a flight attendant. She asked, "How long did it take for you to get back with the Lord?"

"What?" I quickly exclaimed, "I didn't go anywhere. He didn't go anywhere. I couldn't have made it without Him!"

She said, "Well, I had something like that happen to me. I turned my heart away from God. I blamed Him."

I quickly replied, "God didn't do this to me. Man may have turned his back on me. God never turned His back on me." I was able to tell her that God was waiting for her to turn to Him again.

God is my source. He gave me peace. He gave me confidence. He loved me unconditionally when it felt as if no human loved me. He accepted me no matter what I looked like or what clothes I was wearing.

> I heard Him speak back to me, "Great is *thy* faithfulness."

A friend of mine sang one of my favorite songs several years ago. As she sang, "Great Is Thy Faithfulness," God spoke to me through her song.

I thought, "God, man has failed me but You have never failed me. You are *faithful*! God, You *are* faithful. Great is Thy faithfulness."

Once again, in that still small voice, I heard Him speak back to me, "Great is *thy* faithfulness."

I yearned for His voice, those little reassurances that He was always giving me in spite of the confusion and busyness of my life. I desperately needed those encouraging words from Him. I treasure those quiet times with Him when He whispers words of love into my mind and heart.

# #10 Go into His Presence.

When you go into the very presence of God, He engulfs you, and there can be no sin. There is no pain. But you have to go into His presence. You have to spend time with Him and allow Him to heal you.

Press in, and you can go into the wonderful presence of God, where you will be set free and completely healed.

When I went into His presence, God completely healed my heart. During the worst days at the time of the divorce, I felt as if my heart had been taken out of my chest, run through a meat grinder, thrown on the floor, stomped on, and left to die. He picked up a smashed, bleeding, shredded piece of meat. He held it so tenderly and remolded it into a loving, healed heart. He gently placed it back in my chest, put His arms around me, shared His love, and breathed life back into me. Was it perfect at that point? No, but at least it started to beat again.

> God has totally healed my heart. He never left me. He has always been there, and He always will be.

In my chest today beats a heart that God has totally healed! He has healed my heart! He has never left me. He has always been there and will always be there. Do I still cry? Yes, but many times the tears are from happiness. Sometimes my tears are from a heartfelt compassion for others who are still trapped in pain.

Many of you are crying. Perhaps the tears are not coming down your face, but they are flowing in your spirit.

I had constructed a thick wall to protect myself from any additional pain. Because that wall in my own life has come down, I am able to minister God's unconditional love with a greater compassion than ever before.

As I was praying for someone recently, I put my hand on the person's chest to pray, but I couldn't. God was transferring his pain to me. I felt it go out of his heart, through my hand, and into my heart. I said, "I can't pray yet. Wait until I get it all. I want to pray for you with a heart of compassion, a greater understanding than I have ever had before." When I began to pray, I didn't pray from my experience; I prayed from his because I felt all his pain. I prayed, and it left both of us.

Learn what you can from whatever source is opened to you. God can speak through many people in many ways. Ask Him to show you what to do and He will be faithful to answer. Just be open to listen. There is not one and only one way to win the battle. I have shared the strategies that I can readily identify that worked for me. I'm sure there were many other ways He spoke to me to get me to my ultimate destiny. The battle is not over. I know that. But I am certainly much better prepared to fight.

Ephesians 4:27 says, *"Do not give the devil a foothold"* (NIV). Don't give the devil a place in your life: not in your home, not in your heart, not in your emotions, not in your mind. Don't let him come in to influence your heart and mind to destroy you.

We are in a battle and we need to know the correct strategy to win. There are many ways to be healed. Everyone is different. I have shared my battle and what I did to come out victorious. Don't give up. Keep fighting. Find what works for you to get miraculously healed.

Is the ride to the mountaintop easy? No. Is it quick? No.

---

Just as I am free, you can be free!

Just as I am healed, you can be healed!

Just as I can smile again, you can smile again!

---

In fact, every step can take an unbelievable effort; however, one day you will wake up and realize you aren't in the valley any longer. You can look back and wonder who that hurting, broken person was way back in the valley. You will look in the mirror and see a new face, new eyes, and a new determination to live. You will be looking in the mirror and see the love of Jesus looking back at you.

Father, right now, in the name of Jesus, I thank You that these are hearts not of fallow ground. They have been softened and plowed by You for this very moment to receive Your Word that will go into them so they will rise up and be healed. Father, right now, in the name of Jesus, I just thank You for reaching down and taking these broken hearts and healing them.

Put something in your hand that will represent all your pain. Hold it out to God and say,

God, I give this pain to You. I don't want it anymore. It hurts too much. Jesus bore the pain on the cross so I don't have to bear this pain. And, God, You had a broken heart so I don't have to have this broken heart. I don't have to have this defiled heart. I don't have to have this defiled mind or defiled body. Now, I give it to You, in the name of Jesus.

Release whatever you had in your hand and let it fall. Put your hand on your heart and repeat,

Father, in the name of Jesus, I thank You for healing my heart and taking away the pain of the memory. And Father, I thank You that when I talk about anything that has happened to me, I can talk about it from the standpoint of a third person, that You have healed me so much. Father, as I say this, I don't want to glorify the enemy; I want to glorify You for what You have done.

Now, let me pray for you...

Father, Your Word says that a cheerful heart, a healed heart, a well heart, will show in the countenance. I thank You, Father, that I have seen thousands within the body of Christ around the world who have been healed. I have seen them change, and years have just literally fallen away. Instead of a face peeling in the natural, You have peeled away years and years of pain and agony and defeat. Just like an onion, layer after layer after layer has fallen away so that not only the "true them" can shine through, but also the true You can shine through them.

Father, I thank You that You are going to give them wisdom as to who to be around. Not those people who are negative and speaking words that are not of You. Right now, in the name of Jesus, I thank You that You have given us clean hearts. Hearts that beat for You and only for You.

Father, I thank You for Your Word. I thank You for the Word that comforts us today, that leads us on, that tells us what we need to do in times when we have fallen away from what we should have done. Father, You are there to guide us and to help us and to bless us. Father, we thank You for that right now, in Jesus' name.

We thank You that You are the rod and the staff that does comfort us, that does guide us. As we go through various circumstances in our lives, Father, You are there. You are there to comfort and guide us in all circumstances, not just some, but *all* circumstances. As we live for You, our lives will be blessed. We thank You for Your anointing on the Word. We thank You for Your very presence every minute of the day. We thank You for the miracles that You are going to do.

You say,

Father, thank You for healing my heart. Touch me and make me whole. Amen.

Chapter Six

# Blessings and Miracles

T wo days after my divorce was final, I went to the doctor. I had found a lump on my left breast, almost under my arm. Following a mammogram, they diagnosed possible breast cancer. My first thought was, *What outfit should I wear to go with a white casket covered with pink roses?* I mentally slapped myself. *What am I thinking?* The enemy comes to steal, kill, and destroy. (See John 10:10.) He wanted me dead. He didn't want me out ministering. He didn't want me on television. He didn't want me to travel around the world teaching, healing, and laying hands on the sick.

It would have been so easy to just check out. "Praise God, I have breast cancer and I can go home to be with Jesus." It would have been a whole lot easier than experiencing what I went through—emotionally, financially, and in every area of my life—for the next several years. But that's not what God wanted. He didn't want me to give up. He wanted me to regroup and do what He had called me to do.

I felt like giving up at first, but I didn't. I prayed, and my parents agreed with me on the phone. I didn't have a mastectomy, and I didn't have anything removed by a surgeon, either. The next set of mammograms and sonograms were clear. I did have a biopsy, and it showed healthy tissue. I go back to be checked annually. However, God healed me. He removed every bit of cancer.

About a year after the original diagnosis, I went back to the doctor. I was there hours upon end. Testing, sonogram, mammogram, sonogram, mammogram. They kept repeating tests and checking things. I felt as if they were never going to release me. Of course, I feared something was wrong. I wasn't looking forward to the results.

My daughter Melody called and said, "Hi, Mom, what are you doing?"

I said, "I'm still here! There's evidently a problem. They aren't letting me go."

She said, "Oh, Mom, it must be something else."

There had to be a problem. They were keeping me for some reason.

My mind immediately filled with negative thoughts. *The cancer is back.*

*Okay, this is great. I can take the easy way out. Sometimes, the call of God on my life is so hard.*

*I just can't make it any further. God, it would be easier to check out.*

*The girls are taken care of financially. They are old enough now. I have plenty of life insurance. They don't really need me.*

I'm being honest with you. I had myself in the grave. That was my first thought. If you have ever been diagnosed with cancer, that's exactly where your mind goes. The enemy kept feeding me all kinds of lies. He will do the same to you.

I had to stand up and rebuke those thoughts. You have to do the same.

My spirit man within me had to rise up and yell at me, "You are going to live and not die."

God was telling me I would live and not die. I had to decide to "choose life." (See Deuteronomy 30:19.) I had to wake up my spirit and say, "I will live and not die. I will declare the works of the Lord. (See Psalm 118:17.) If God healed me the first time I was diagnosed with cancer, then He can do it again. I will live and not die. I will live and not die."

> I had to choose life.
> I will live and not die.
> I choose life! I will
> live and not die!

The X-ray technician finally came in to "check more angles." There weren't any more angles to check; they had done so many already. She finally came in and said, "There is a problem."

I said, "I kind of figured that."

So I gripped the examining table, preparing myself to hear the worst.

She said, "Yes, we do have a problem, and we are not happy. We have your new mammogram here and your previous mammogram over here. Your name and social security number is the same on both, but it is not the same breast. The problem is, we can't find the problem. All the scar tissue, all the evidence of the biopsy, is gone."

That had never happened before. Usually, they ask you to return after a few months or years to check everything again. Instead, they said they didn't need to see me again. They couldn't understand what happened.

It was an exciting time. God is so good!

Who wanted me dead? The enemy. Why? Because of what is going on in my life now. The stakes were high; he came after me with an unbelievable vengeance because he wanted me snuffed out. He wants you out of the picture, too. That's why it is so hard for people to come to anointed meetings, such as a healing school. That's why some get sick the night before a special meeting or convention. The enemy doesn't want anyone to hear the Word of God. He doesn't want anyone to get free. He feeds everyone lies and more lies. Who do you listen to? Who do you believe?

My spirit man had to rise up and say, "This far and no more. I am going on no matter what. God wants to use me. Nothing, certainly not the lying, stinking devil, is going to stop me from doing what God is calling me to do. Amen."

Someone came to me some time ago and said, "You will always have the scar, the pain."

"No!" God has healed me. I look at a picture of the "old Joan" from years ago and I don't even remember her. She is dead.

"But you'll always have that scar."

"No!" No, Jesus came not only to heal me, but also to make me *"every whit whole"* (John 7:23 KJV). God not only healed me of the breast cancer, but He also healed the scar from the biopsy. He not only healed me, but He also made me every whit whole.

I felt I was worthless and meant nothing to anybody. I felt like trash that had been used and then thrown away. God had to prove me wrong. However, I had to be willing to be proven wrong. He took care of me. He took care of my girls.

God will take care of your every need, as well. And He does know what you need. He also knows what you want; however, He doesn't promise to provide all your wants and desires. Interestingly, as you walk closely with Him, your desires become His desires. Believe in Him and His provision and He will provide. Today, you may have enough to get by, but not enough for the things you want to do. Your thoughts may be, *If I give that then I can't make my house or car payment.* Believe God that your house and cars are paid in full. Use your provisions as He directs and you will always have enough. If a church or ministry needs an extra $5000, you should be able to freely give it without a second thought. He wants us to walk in abundance.

I had expected way too little. I had limited God. He had miraculously gotten me into a beautiful house, so why couldn't He just pay it off? It was a miracle to get into it; I might as well expect another miracle to also pay it off. I am not going to limit God anymore. I expect my bills to be paid. I don't want to be concerned about the house payment every month. Although I believe God to meet all my needs, I would rather believe God for more miracles instead of wasting time worrying and praying for finances to pay the bills every month.

Often, we hear about believing God for finances and His provisions. Praise God, He always comes through for us. However, we can't limit him to providing only finances and things. He freely gives us His healing touch, also. How often have we "put up with" an ache or pain instead of going to Him for healing? We don't want to bother Him unless it is a "life threatening" situation. We often have a need for healing in many areas of our lives, especially in certain areas that we often try to hide or deny.

God wants to customize your healing process. As you are open to Him, You will understand more and more of what He wants to do in your life. He will show you those areas that need His touch, just as He showed me.

For instance, God hit me in the area of pride. I didn't realize I had a problem with pride; however, God showed me that I did. I had to repent. It hurt at first, but it was so exciting to see how God literally turned everything around.

Somebody came to me from the food closet, which collected and distributed free food to those in need, and said, "I want to give you some food."

I thought to myself, "I don't need food from the food closet. I am not going to belittle myself by accepting food from the food closet." So I told that person, "No!"

> As you are open to God, you will understand more and more of what He wants to do in your life.

When somebody offers you free food, it is hard to swallow. Some can handle it, some can't. And God really dealt with me. He said, "I want to bless you. I want to bless you with food so the money can go toward something else." If someone gave me money toward my electric bill, I was okay. But, if someone wanted to give me food so I could use the money toward the electric bill, I was embarrassed.

One day, someone delivered a truckload of groceries. Hundreds and hundreds of dollars' worth of groceries plus a check for $150 for milk and fresh food. We were so blessed. I was nearly speechless. All I could say was, "Praise God. Thank You, Jesus!" And I cried. God was so good!

"How are you possibly making it on that little bit of money?" My CPA told me time and again that I would not make it with the little money I was earning. He advised me to stop tithing and giving offerings. Did I stop giving to God? No! I changed CPAs. I know what works!

I told myself I could take a little bit from here and a little bit from there, trying to make ends meet, or I could recognize there is all this room for God to bless me as long as I tithe and give my offerings. I called in my harvest. I seeded and seeded and seeded in order to receive a rich harvest. I got saved at twelve years of age and I have always tithed. And I have never gone without. He takes care of me.

God proved Himself again and again. Another time, I didn't have money for groceries. I sent Melody to the store with my credit card because I didn't have the cash. Most of us have been there and done that. I am no different from anyone else. I am not superhuman. I don't recommend using a credit card when you don't have the money for something; but we needed the groceries.

As I sent Melody to the store, I said, "God, I don't know what You are going to do, but I know You will make up the difference."

While Melody was at the grocery store, I went to the mailbox. Inside was an envelope from a friend. He was a single man who was holding down three jobs to maintain his living expenses. Inside the envelope was a check for $125. His note said, "God laid it on my heart that you needed this money more than I did this week. I would rather go without than to know you and your children had to go without." I cried. My friend was being obedient to His heavenly Father.

I immediately prayed God would pour a great big blessing over my friend.

So often I need another blessing, another miracle, from my heavenly Father. I walk in faith that He will supply everything in every area of my life. You could say I have learned the hard way that His way is truly the easy way. My way fails miserably. His way was and is so glorious. I had to lay my finances and worry on the altar. My worrying didn't help.

Three of the girls were in college. Miraculously, government grants and scholarships came through to help finance their education. Spice was a junior at Oral Roberts University and was determined to complete her senior year there. In the natural, this was very difficult because the cost of tuition at a private university can be very high. We received the letter from the school outlining the amount that she would need to complete her final year. We prayed! She continued on with her plans. Before the school year even started, the government came through with $4500 and she received several scholarships, including one for her scholastic achievements.

His way is truly the easy way.

Spice graduated from ORU in 2001 with honors and went on to medical school. She became a doctor of naturopathy in 2006. She is a great resource for me. When I have a question about a disease, she can explain the disease process and what treatment is recommended. She then adds, "And this is how you pray for it!"

God was so good! He was so faithful!

Pray right now and give this area of your life to the Lord:

Father, I lay my finances on Your altar. I cannot fix them. I will be faithful with my tithes and offerings. I trust You to make up the difference. Thank You, in Jesus' name.

Occasionally, I have been in services where the prophetic word is exactly what I needed, but the finger wasn't pointing at me. I was on the other side of the room. I simply said, "God, it doesn't matter where the evangelist's finger pointed, I receive that financial breakthrough; I receive that breakthrough in my ministry. I receive. I receive. My 'expectors' are up in the name of Jesus."

I do expect Him to act. And He has. Have things changed? Yes. So many things have miraculously become new.

# Chapter Seven

# Reinforce Your Foundation

C onsider this list of miracles: God healed me of a broken heart, betrayal, the pain of divorce, depression, obesity, low self-esteem, breast cancer, and financial ruin, just to name a few. Can you imagine what it is like never to be wanted by your husband? And believe it was your fault? Being called "stupid" by all your teachers? They told me, "You will never amount to anything. You'll be washing dishes to survive."

People told me I would never live through the situation. I did, yet I'm going stronger than ever before. God came in, cleaned me up, healed me, and set my feet on higher ground. I am doing more for Him today than ever before. I am happier than I have ever been in my entire life. About a year after the divorce, I started dating. I had never dated in my life. Suddenly, I had gentlemen taking me to dinner all the time. For several months, I didn't pay for a meal.

After twenty-five years of not being good enough, I discovered I was wanted and desired. Men wanted to talk to me and laugh at my jokes. They wanted to open doors for me and treat me like a precious jewel. It built up my self-esteem. It was exciting. It was fun.

After several months, I went to God with a question. "I want to know if You want me to be married. I don't want to date the rest of my life, even though it was a great experience. If I am to get married, please show me. If not, then remove this desire from me."

One evening, I was preparing a message from Isaiah 61 that tells how God healed the brokenhearted. I looked down and read, *"You shall be called by a new name, which the mouth of the LORD will name"* (Isaiah 62:2).

I shut my Bible and said, "Thank You very much. I look forward to meeting him."

God says, "Just wait on Me and allow Me to bring the blessings into your life that I have reserved for you."

At that point, God said, "You have had your fun. I want you to stop dating. Just wait on Me and allow Me to bring him into your life. You have done what you wanted to do. Now let Me do what I am going to do."

I simply said, "Yes, Sir!"

I knew His way would be the perfect way. I just had to listen to Him and follow His direction. I am known for being an organizer, a "woman of action." I do things; I don't sit back and wait for someone else to act. However, I had to learn to wait on Him, to do things His way without question.

Moses spent forty years in the wilderness with the Israelites. Forty long years. Why were they there for so long? First of all, their grumbling words. "Poor me. Why am I here?" It took a week, at most, to get from Egypt into the Promised Land; however, it took the Israelites forty years. The second reason was that they didn't trust their leader. They complained, "What's for dinner? Manna again? Pheasant? Yuk!" You name it, they complained about it. They hadn't learned the power of their words.

Watch your words and do not grumble. When you fight the battle saying, "Woe is me. Why is this happening to me?" you will go around the block another dozen times. As for me, I want out of the desert as fast as I can. I had to look up to God and think positively. I had to put my hand in His hand and, in total submission and obedience, follow Him.

One day, I was talking on the phone to a friend from Azle, Texas, who was visiting in Dallas. Suddenly, she said, "I am lost. I have no idea where I am. I am going around in circles. I have to stop and look at the map."

She looked at the map, got a general idea of where she needed to go, drove in that direction, and saw the freeway that she needed to be on. She suddenly said, "I can see where I need to be, but I just can't get there."

We prayed. She got on the right track and finally said, "I'm on the freeway. I am on my way home."

Sometimes, you can see where you need to be but you just can't get there. What do you need to do? Pray. When you have been in a whirlwind situation and feel lost, it is exciting to find you are headed in the right direction—the direction God wants you to follow. Then you are in God's perfect will, exactly where He wants you to go, exactly where He wants you to be. That's so important.

Do you want to stay where you are? I don't. What are you doing to change that?

Most of us know the name and face of Arnold Schwarzenegger. He is strong, well built, muscular, and has no obvious extra weight. What does it take to have a physique somewhere between flabby and "almost" Arnold?

Let's say that you decide one day, "I'm going to the gym, and I'll come out looking really buff." So you go to the gym, work out for an hour, and go back home to look in the mirror. "Yeah, it only took an hour, and I look just like Arnold!"

No! That's not what happens. You have to go day after day after day—hour after hour after hour. You have to concentrate. You have to push food to the side, your job to the side, people to the side, sacrificing everything in order to meet your goal.

If you want to change yourself spiritually, you have to make a serious long-term commitment to make some changes. You need to do whatever you can do to reach your goal. To get stronger, you need to spend hours and hours a day in the "spiritual" gym, exercising every spiritual muscle. If you are weak in the area of finances, you read books about finances, read the Scriptures about finances, and talk to people who have had incredible financial miracles in their lives. If you need healing, you find books about how to get healed, listen to His servants teach about healing, feed your spirit with food from the Word on healing, and talk to people who have experienced miraculous healings.

Believe God's promises and don't listen to the enemy's lies. How do you withstand the attacks of the enemy? By having a strong foundation. Has something happened to make you think, *This isn't fair! I didn't deserve this. Why did this happen?*

Stop worrying. You may never know why. You can dwell on the problem forever and get nowhere because you cannot see the whole picture. Only God knows the complete effect of your life or actions. The Bible tells you the enemy is trying to separate you from God while God wants you to draw closer to Him. The battle is not really yours, but God's. But you must know how to survive the battles.

Next, you need to work on the foundation. Proverbs 10:25 says, *"The righteous has an everlasting foundation."*

Visualize a mountaintop as I describe the scene. Maybe you have been to Colorado or Alaska. What do you see there? Snow. Green trees. Animals. Deer. Elk. It seems you can see forever on a clear day. Birds. Airplanes. Gorgeous, unimaginable things. God's incredibly beautiful creation.

> You need a strong foundation to survive the winds of the enemy.

Suddenly, a blizzard comes. If you are in the protected valley, you will not be affected. What about the mountaintop? The winds blow at 50 to 125 miles per hour. If you don't have a strong foundation or protection, you aren't going to survive. The winds are the enemy, and they are going to blow. That is a fact, a certainty. It is going to happen. What do you do? You have to have a firm foundation, built on the Word of God. You need a close relationship with God to keep you safe through the stormy winds on the mountaintops of life.

I was born and raised in Miami, Florida. Whenever the weatherman announced an impending hurricane, we planned a hurricane party. TV and radio stations would broadcast the storm's progress twenty-four hours a day for several days before landfall. Their warnings were frequent and early, giving us time to prepare. We gathered together plenty of food, beverages, bottled water, and batteries. We buckled down, boarded up, and prepared for the big storm. We were safely tucked away in our protected surroundings waiting for the winds to blow.

"Is it coming this way?"

"No. It's going this way."

"Oh, it's changed again."

The location of landfall, the point of most destruction, is never a sure thing until it actually happens. The wind, the rain, and the atmosphere all change rapidly in such a tumultuous situation. What makes a hurricane move toward a particular location? The low pressure. Landfall is estimated, or "guesstimated," while the warning sirens blow and cars jammed with people and their belongings attempt to escape the destructive winds and rain.

> When you are connected to God, you are safe and secure under the shadow of His wings.

When I have watched TV, I don't remember ever hearing any spiritual forecasts. There is no spiritual weather channel. No one is going to run up a special flag or blow a siren to warn us of impending spiritual disaster. When you are low spiritually, you draw the attacks in your direction. When you are down, the enemy will come in to hit you, knocking you down further. His goal is to destroy you. Are you going to allow it? You don't have to.

Get connected so tightly to God that you are secure and protected under His wings. When you are sheltered, protected, and spiritually strong, the storms, the attacks, will not destroy you. You may experience them, but they are not going to knock you down. They will not paralyze you or knock you out of the game.

*In all your ways acknowledge Him, and He shall direct your paths.* (Proverbs 3:6)

*Knowing that the testing of your faith produces patience.* (James 1:3)

Everyone is tested. Everyone has trials and tribulations. I have lived through them. I survived. You can, too. If you are going to experience them, you must be prepared for them. Tests develop character. When a test is thrown at you, just answer the questions and go on.

I didn't want to dwell on that test for forty years like Moses and the Israelites. I wanted to go on with Him. I had other things to do besides concentrating on my well-being. I had to stay spiritually healthy. God had called me to a worldwide ministry. I couldn't do that if I was wallowing in "Woe is me" all day long, thinking, *Oh, I don't have enough of this. I don't have enough emotional stamina. I don't have enough love. I don't have this or that.*

No more excuses. That may be where I once was, but that's not where I am today. I am fired up with what God has called me to do.

Has God promised you some things, given you ideas for things you want to do? God has told me so much, it blows me away. One morning, I was reading in Proverbs. I love Proverbs. I need its wisdom in every area of my life. If you need love, go to John, Ephesians, and Corinthians, but if you need wisdom, go to Proverbs. There are so many incredible Scriptures. So many promises.

Suddenly, I thought, *This is not where I need to be reading today.* I couldn't get into it at all. I use my *New Living Translation* of the Bible at home for my daily devotions, and I saw all the sticky notes that I had previously placed to highlight special revelations from God. I thought, *I am going to read all the blessings of God that He has promised me. I haven't read these in awhile.*

> The Bible is full of incredible Scriptures that hold promises for you. Go to God and claim them for your life.

One by one, I turned to those Scriptures. As I read several of them, I said, "God, I don't see this happening in my life. You promised this to me," as I tapped my finger on my Bible.

I flipped to the next note. "God, You see that little sticky note? That's a great word. You promised that to me. I don't see it in my life."

It was just Him and me in the bedroom as I continued, "You promised that to me in April. I dated it. I don't see that in my life. I don't see the doors of my ministry opening up. At least not as fast as I want it to." I went through all the promises and said, "These Scriptures blessed me today, but I don't see them in my life. I don't see the doors opening up like You have shown me. I have seeded for that. I have believed You for that. You have told me these things are going to happen. So be it."

No one likes to patiently wait for something. I was no different. I was getting impatient with God that morning. "God, I don't see it. I want to see it. I want something to confirm that I am doing what I am supposed to do and that the dream that You have given me is coming to pass." I got mad and told Him what I needed to hear. I stood on what God told me to do.

What was He going to do? He was going to prove Himself.

Four hours later, while I was at work, the phone rang. "We would like to have you on our television program." This Dallas-based Christian TV station beams its programs around the world to millions of homes. I was so excited that I danced around my office and my coworkers. I was hysterically yelling, laughing, and crying all at the same time.

Ever since that morning when I reminded God of what He had promised me (as if He really needed to be reminded), I often need to be reminded to expect more. Several other invitations came in shortly after that. The doors were opening.

I chose to reach forward. I chose to forget those things that happened before. I want what God has prepared for me.

*"If we hope for what we do not see, we eagerly wait for it with perseverance"* (Romans 8:25).

As I said before, God gave me this word, which is still posted on my refrigerator and my computer: "I have it all worked out. You just have to walk it out."

There are situations in your life that you have to deal with; you have to walk through them while holding on to Him and listening to His direction. Whatever it is, you will make it if you are determined to make it. You must be willing for God to use the situations in your life to make you better.

*"Yet in all these things we are more than conquerors through Him who loved us"* (Romans 8:37). It is not because we love Him, but because He loved us that we are more than conquerors.

> *And we know that all things work together for good to those who love God, to those who are the called according to His purpose.* (Romans 8:28)

The word *"all"* is a very, very strong word. It doesn't say "some of the time" or "some of the things." It says *all* things. *All* means including everything and excluding nothing. Did God cause all my problems? No. But He is going to take them and use them to His advantage and mine. Did He cause your problems? Of course not; however, He will use them for your good if you only allow Him to work in your life.

Another promise that I love to claim is this: *"I can do all things through Christ who strengthens me"* (Philippians 4:13).

There is that word again—*all.*

> *(For the LORD your God is a merciful God), He will not forsake you nor destroy you, nor forget the covenant of your fathers which He swore to them.* (Deuteronomy 4:31)

You have a choice. What are you going to do? There is an

opportunity for you to do more for God. What is keeping you from doing more for Him?

*But thanks be to God, who gives us the victory through our Lord Jesus Christ.* (1 Corinthians 15:57)

Even though there are situations that you must go through, you are more than a conqueror. You can do *all* things through Christ who strengthens you.

## All things!

# Chapter Eight

# Are You Determined to Be Healed?

I had absolutely no idea how dependent I was on my husband. For years and years, I lived as though I could not survive without that man. But God has healed me of that abnormal dependence. You may also be dependent on somebody else, whether it is your parents, your spouse, or someone or something else. You need to depend on and trust in your spouse, but not be so dependent that you can't even breathe without them.

The only One you should be totally dependent on is God. You can trust Him 1000 percent to always do His best for you. His love is unconditional, not dependent on your behavior. He is always there for you and will not desert you. He will not call you names or make you feel ugly. He will tell you how very special you are to Him while He fights your battles for you and protects you. You simply have to believe in Him and allow Him to work through you. You have to trust Him implicitly to guide you through life.

God wants you to be a survivor and, through Him, you can be. Are you going to make it on your own? No. You have to depend on Him. You have to walk with Him in a greater way. You have to know Him better than any friend, any person that you have ever known. He already knows you better than you want anybody else to know you. In addition, during the process, you will find out more about yourself.

I have made some major decisions about myself—self-improvement like you wouldn't believe. I want to be the best person that I can be, for God to use. I don't want to be His second choice. I don't want Him to skip over me to go to somebody else. I want to be used by God.

What did I have to do to be chosen? Did I have to be perfect? No, thank God! Do I have to work on perfecting myself on a daily basis? Yes. Have I arrived? No.

The Scripture says,

*Brethren, I do not count myself to have apprehended; but one thing I do, forgetting those things which are behind and reaching forward to those things which are ahead.* (Philippians 3:13)

I don't think I have apprehended, or arrived at, where I want to be. Thank God, I am not where I want to be. I know He has a whole lot more for me. He could not have used me the way I was a few years ago. I had to want to be healed completely so I could do anything and everything that He has called me to do.

I want to be ready both spiritually and physically. I want to be ready in every area because I want to be used by God.

The blessings of God will overtake you.

In the workplace? Yes. In my neighborhood? Yes. And if God calls me to minister somewhere on the other side of town or the other side of the world, I need to be ready, willing, and able.

*And all these blessings shall come on thee, and overtake thee, if thou shalt hearken unto the voice of the LORD thy God.* (Deuteronomy 28:2 KJV)

*"Bring all the tithes into the storehouse so there will be enough food in my Temple. If you do," says the LORD Almighty, "I will open the windows of heaven for you. I will pour out a blessing so great you won't have enough room to take it in! Try it! Let me prove it to you!"* (Malachi 3:10 TLB)

*Trouble chases sinners, while blessings chase the righteous!* (Proverbs 13:21 TLB)

The windows of heaven have opened up in my life. Scripture says that the blessings will chase me and overtake me. It does not say the temptations, trials, and tests are running to overtake me. The blessings of God are running after the righteous to overtake them.

When the storms of life come, there are three main things that we can do.

*#1 Rebuke the storm.* Rebuke the situation, and it will flee.

*#2 Walk it out with Him.* If the storm doesn't abate when you speak to it, know that you can walk through the storm. God is there beside you and He will keep you protected even as the wind and rain swirl around you.

*#3 Wait.* If the storm still continues to rage, know that this is something that you must go through in your life, but it will not last forever. Wait in faith for it to end, and know that God is perfecting you through the trial.

For example, it is pouring rain outside. You can rebuke it, in the name of Jesus, and it stops, sometimes. Or, you can walk it out and get wet on the way to the car. Or, you can camp out for the next several hours and wait for the rain to stop and the clouds to disappear. There are several ways to handle storms and opportunities.

I have believed God for the windows of heaven to open up and they are doing just that.

God gave me a key, a well-known Scripture. It is the key to what God wants in my life, a key that will open up everything in every area. What is the key? What is the key to financial freedom? What is the key that will open the windows of heaven to blessings in your life? What is the key that will bless your family? It is contained in one Scripture. You have heard this Scripture a thousand times. If you remember nothing else, remember this.

*Beloved, I wish above all things that thou mayest prosper and be in health, even as thy soul prospereth.*                              (3 John 1:2 KJV)

With that verse, He is saying everything that I have written here. "I wish above all things that have been in the Bible before this, or will be after this, I wish above *all* things that you will prosper." He wants us to *prosper.* Isn't that exciting? He doesn't want us on "Barely Get Along Street." And not only does He want all of us to prosper in the financial realm, but He also wants us to be in perfect health.

If I was sick and complaining, "Oh, arthritis. My knee is hurting again!" you wouldn't want to listen to me. You wouldn't believe my testimony that He is supplying my every need. God wants you in good health. Receive it. He wants you to prosper in every area of your life. Just financially? No, His blessings will pour over your family, relationships, friendships, jobs, and finances. Expect them. Receive them.

What is the key to having our souls prosper? Get into the Word. Praise Him. Worship Him. Listen to CDs, tapes, and teachings everywhere you can and anytime you can.

> The key to having your soul prosper is to get into the Word, and praise and worship the Creator.

I played every praise and worship CD that I could find. I listened to every tape series about how to heal a broken heart. I did whatever I could do to make sure I was feeding my wounded spirit and broken heart. I asked for and received prayer every time I could from His servants.

I went into His presence.

Others may be content hearing about the presence of God or talking about the presence of God, but you need to *experience* the presence of God. You have to press in.

Read His Word, study His teachings, feed your spirit with His spiritual food. Then, no matter what happens, you will be so filled up with the Word of God that the windows of heaven will open up for you like you have never before experienced. God is opening up the windows of heaven financially for me and is literally blowing me away.

Melody was taking music lessons and asked one day, "Well, do I need to cut back and take the lessons maybe once a month?"

I said, "No, God is blessing us financially so you can continue." In the natural, a few months before, there would have been no way. But she went on to develop one of the gifts that God had given her.

God wants to bless her, God wants to bless me, and God wants to bless you. What is the key? Doing everything you can to develop your relationship with God. In order to learn about and get to know another person, you spend time communicating with them about family, cares, joys, and victories. It is the same thing with Him. You have to spend time with God to learn about Him. You have to learn about His Son. Spend time in the Word. Spend time in praise and worship.

Again, I spend many hours at home working in my office. I play praise and worship music as I work. In other words, I worship as I work. Take advantage of your time. For instance, I run errands in my car while listening to teaching or music. I love it. Listening to tapes and CDs has helped me as well as blessed those around me. Those blessings have multiplied and rippled through others.

God wants to do so much in my life and in yours. So much time has been taken from me. So much time has been stolen from you. He wants to redeem my time, and He will redeem your time. There have been times where I have been dry spiritually. It has happened to you, also. He wants to redeem that time and turn that around. Be willing to allow Him to take complete control over your life. Let Him redeem every minute, every second that the enemy has stolen from you. Receive His blessings. My arms are open and anticipating His blessings all the time. I expect His blessings. I receive them daily. You must expect and receive everything He has for you and your life.

Everyone knows Psalm 23, and can probably quote it; however, I am going to personalize it.

> The Lord is my Shepherd. I shall not want. He makes me to lie down in green and cranberry pastures (the colors of my bedroom). He leads me beside the still waters. He restores my soul. He leads me in the path of righteousness for His name's sake. Yea, though I crawled through the valley of the shadow of death, I feared no evil because my God was with me.

There were times when I could not walk. There were times when there were only two footsteps, not four. There were so many times when He had to carry me, and He did. He carried me through everything. He will do the same for you.

Envision the woman mentioned in the Bible who had bled for twelve years. In the world today, if a woman bleeds for four or five days, she is tired and weak and can become anemic. For twelve years, this lady bled. Even though the Bible didn't say she was anemic, I am sure she was so weak she could barely even get out of her own home. However, she woke up one morning determined that she was going to be healed that day. She turned her computer on and found out where Jesus was going to be, hopped in her car, and drove to the meeting.

That's not the way it was. She didn't get a flier from the church announcing a meeting time or place. She didn't get any news on TV or radio. There was no way for her to know where He would be. She was determined and had her "expectors" up. She knew that day was the day for her breakthrough. She crawled out of bed, crawled to a nearby chair, pushed herself upright, and left her house leaning on any objects within reach. She probably fell many times on her way to find Jesus. As she crawled, she was determined to get to Him.

She finally saw Him in the distance surrounded by a huge crowd of people. In her weakened condition, this lady was so determined that she made it through all the people to touch the hem of His garment. She reached her goal. She pushed through. She received her healing. (See Matthew 9:20–22.)

> You need determination to fight through the crowd and touch the hem of His garment for your healing.

If you want to be healed in any area of your life, you need that same determination. If you want to be debt free, you have to have that kind of determination. If you want to be healed mentally, spiritually, physically, emotionally, or any other way, you have to have that same kind of determination against all odds. Even against people who tell you healing will take another five to seven years. You may have to fight every inch of the way to touch the hem of His garment.

When I touched the hem of His garment in the spirit realm, He healed me. Not only healed me but also made me whole. He removed all the scars. I experienced so many miracles. He is still restoring things over and above and beyond anything I can ask or seek or imagine. (See Ephesians 3:20.) He will do the same for you. He will do the same for your friends and family, also.

If someone you know is going through a bad situation, be there for them. If they have a need, tell them to give you a call twenty-four hours a day. So what if they wake you up for a night or two. They probably haven't slept in weeks. Sacrifice a little bit. You have to make the decision that you cannot quit and you will not quit, no matter what. Help them make the same decision. Be a testimony to them and for them. Learn what He wants for your life and then share it with someone else. Be His hands; emulate Him, imitate Him, and share His love.

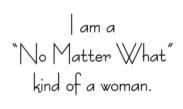

I am a "No Matter What" kind of a woman.

I did a ladies seminar a few years ago. I spoke on "I am a 'No Matter What' kind of a woman." That's what I am. No matter what the enemy wants to do to me, it doesn't make any difference anymore. Because "No Matter What," it will become one more platform, one more area where I can stand up and say, "God's healed me of this. God's healed me of that. He came through again in that situation."

My children have their own testimonies of healing. Once they realized that the breakup of our home and marriage wasn't my fault, they saw the truth and recognized the lies told about me. They turned around, and God is healing each of them in marvelous ways.

The hardest thing for them to understand was why their father married me in the first place. Why did he use me? Why did he stay married to me during his infidelity? Why didn't he just get a divorce and go on with his lifestyle rather than continue it during the marriage? These are questions that will probably never be answered.

One day, the children wanted us to sit down for one more meal as a family. I agreed to the plan. You say, "How could you do that?" Well, he and I were at opposite ends of the table. His partner was there with him. I had all my children. His mother, who still loves me to this day, was there. I didn't have to talk with him and everyone appeared to have a good time.

Afterward, I told someone, "It's amazing what we will do for our children."

How could I do that? Because I was so healed.

The next day, the children started planning the next family get-together. I told them, "The next time will be at your wedding." I had done the dinner, and that was enough to prove that I had gotten stronger.

Thank You, God.

You are so faithful.

Thank You for Your healing touch.

"God, let me touch others with Your love."

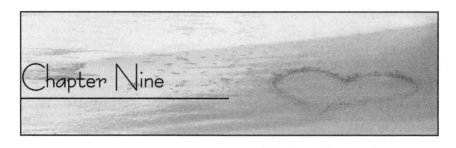

# Chapter Nine

# How Can I Forgive?

People who meet me today know I have no resentment, no bitterness or unforgiveness, left in my heart. It didn't happen overnight. It happened over a period of time, although the majority of it was actually gone within the first year. According to the Word of God, you must forgive the person or people who have hurt you.

Unforgiveness is the poison that we drink hoping the other person will get sick. As I have ministered to people for years, I have heard such things as, "Why am I sick when he is the one who did that to me?" He had asked for forgiveness and was free. She said she had forgiven him; however, she really had not. She held bitterness and resentment through the years, which then showed up in her body and was destroying her health.

We have all heard that we must forgive another person for hurting us. Actually doing it is another matter. However, even as children, when we got our feelings hurt, we had to "get over it" and go on. Eventually, we wanted our friend's companionship more than we wanted to brood on the insult or hurt. In essence, even at a young age, we were learning to forgive. We just didn't hear or use that word. We had to "share," "learn to get along," "compromise," "socialize." There are many other words to use, such as "give and take," "choose your battles," or "bargain."

We wanted our way then and often we want our way even as adults. If someone else sees things a different way or acts in a manner contrary to our expectations, we have a choice. We can accept what the person does, ignore it, or react. If it directly affects us, we can choose to get upset about it, try to change the person, or learn from it.

No one has the perfect answer for anything. There are many avenues to get to a destination or goal. Maybe ours isn't the fastest or most direct route, just the one we learned as a child.

> Unforgiveness is the poison that we drink hoping that the other person will get sick.

Understanding, love, and faith all have very important parts in communication. Sometimes we speak to people and wonder if we are even speaking the same language. From experience, I can honestly say this often happens between husbands and wives. For example, we all have our own "love languages." When I was first married, the term *love language* hadn't been defined. I thought love was love.

Years before the subjects of "love languages," "right and left brain motivations of the sexes," "personalities," "premarital counseling," or the myriad of studies to help us understand other people, our attraction to the opposite sex was often superficial and physical rather than based on other levels of compatibility, especially in the spiritual aspects of a relationship.

So many mismatched couples suffered through years of miserable marriage because they were quick to "hook up" in the first place. Or perhaps their goals were so divergent that they grew apart. Their interests varied widely and they couldn't find common ground on which to maintain a compatible relationship. I used to counsel couples with such problems. Never in a million years did I believe I would find myself in the same situation, searching for relief from such pain.

As we grow older, some childish, selfish demands overtake and control our lives. On the other side of the proverbial coin, those who in their childhoods have had to submit to others' desires in order to find any peace and satisfaction (who have become codependent) continue to do so in adult relationships, also. They feel their desires and wants are not worthy, not necessary, not valuable, or not important.

Our complex lives have so many facets, we often have many "faces" or "personalities" depending on the environment or the people we are currently around.

In addition, what seems negative to one person may be considered positive to another. We may get insulted and the other person doesn't realize what he or she has done. Honest communication between people has to be developed as well as learned in most cases. Respect for the hopes and dreams and goals of another must be a two-way street and not a selfish "my way or the highway" stand.

In my case, how could I forgive? I do realize that there are always two sides to every story or marriage. He wasn't all to blame and neither was I. We both made choices.

Unfortunately, I didn't, I couldn't, understand what he needed or wanted. I couldn't meet his needs. He didn't understand what I needed, either. I tried to be a good wife and mother. I truly believe I was the best wife and mother that I knew how to be. What he wanted, however, I couldn't give or become. I had to accept that I could not succeed in that area.

At first, all I could feel was the pain, the agony, the physical and emotional manifestations of betrayal and desertion. Eventually, I realized and understood that God had to remove him from my life in order for my growth and development into what He wanted me to become. In spite of all the negative comments and put-downs, I hung on to the dream God had given me when I was younger. I knew He was going to use me. I knew I was His child. I knew that God had great things ahead for me. In spite of the barricades within my path, I didn't lose sight of the end goal.

In my flesh I didn't want to forgive him. I wanted to do something to let him know how much he had hurt me and the girls. Would it have done any good? No, because he didn't understand before or after. From his perspective, I was the problem hindering him from his goal of happiness. From my side, he was the problem. An impasse had been reached. Today, I know God had His hand on me right in the middle of the mess. All the while, He was leading me out of the situation that held me back from His perfect will.

Through all that I learned and experienced, God can now use me to minister to millions of hurting people around the world. I can minister with total compassion and understanding because I was once there. I have felt the anguish and then the victory as God healed me.

*But as for you, you meant evil against me; but God meant it for good, in order to bring it about as it is this day, to save many people alive.* (Genesis 50:20)

No one likes painful change. Happy, blissful change is great, wonderful, marvelous. Marriage, birth, and reconciliation all bring change, pain, and then great happiness. However, losing a job, finances, home, or family doesn't seem to have any positive aspects on the surface. Through these experiences, we do grow and change. Again, we have the choice to become bitter or better. I choose every day to become better.

I went through the valley; I climbed to the mountaintop. Somewhere along the way, the pain receded as God reminded me of His goal for my life. He had better things for my future than my errant spouse ever had. I had trusted my husband to lead and guide when he was still trying to find himself. I had submitted, served, and been faithful. I truly believe God honored my obedience to my spouse despite the problems.

God will use your painful past if you let Him.

The enemy would like to keep me bitter, angry, in tears, and essentially paralyzed. If I am so wrapped up in the negative, I can never do anything positive for myself, my children, or God. My goal is to be more and more like Jesus. I want to be in God's perfect will. I had to choose to fight against the negative feelings and thoughts that were holding me down. In truth, my spirit had to fight birth pangs to finally emerge into true life. I wanted to live, not just survive. I wanted to grow in God and find peace, love, and joy anew.

Could I forgive? I couldn't in my own strength. I fell to my knees as I turned to God.

The Scriptures direct me to forgive. Jesus forgave His murderers while hanging on the cruel cross of Calvary. (See Luke 23:34.) In such torment and agony, He forgave. If He did it, can't I forgive betrayal also? Again, it is easier said than done. However, if I am to be more like Jesus every day of my life, I have to follow His example. I made the choice. I forgave. There are days I still have to choose to forgive again as a situation arises over the children. I know the enemy would like to drag me back to where I was. But now I recognize it and say, "Praise God, I am free!"

We repeat these words so often: *"Forgive us our debts, as we forgive our debtors"* (Matthew 6:12). In reverse, we are saying, "If we don't forgive others, God won't forgive us." (See verses 14–15.) Unforgiveness blocks our prayers, our communication with our Father. The bitterness, resentment, and emotional pain causes damage to our physical bodies, our relationships with others, and our peace of mind, as well.

It is our choice how to react. Again, we can choose life or death, light or darkness. There are so many factors involved with relationships, such as words spoken, inflections in the voice, attitude of the body, and facial expressions, as well as past history, that can contribute to miscommunication. Even an overheard comment without the context of a full conversation can be used as a weapon between people who usually get along.

*Judge not, and you shall not be judged. Condemn not, and you shall not be condemned. Forgive, and you will be forgiven. Give, and it will be given to you: good measure, pressed down, shaken together, and running over will be put into your bosom. For with the same measure that you use, it will be measured back to you.* (Luke 6:37–38)

*For if you forgive men their trespasses, your heavenly Father will also forgive you. But if you do not forgive men their trespasses, neither will your Father forgive your trespasses.* (Matthew 6:14–15)

When do you know you have truly forgiven the other person who has hurt you, betrayed you, deserted you? When you have truly forgiven, the good memories will outweigh the bad, and the pain of what happened will be gone. Will it happen overnight? Probably not. However, God's love will ease and finally erase the aches and penetrating pain. It will become another experience of your past, one of the things you have learned from and will not repeat. These things allow God to use you to minister to others.

When I look back on the twenty-five years we had together, I now can remember more of the good times we had together, not the bad. He was very smart and could do anything. He taught me so many things through the years of our marriage. I was a sponge and always felt he had the answer to everything. He loved our girls and pushed them much harder than I would have done during their school years. He knew the importance of a good education and was determined that our children were going to do as well as they could in school. They all are achieving good things in their lives and I know his drive and encouragement did have a positive effect on them. He was a good provider. We had a very nice home and were never deprived of the necessities of life.

Someone asked one of my girls, "It must have been hard growing up with your dad."

Her response was great. "It wasn't all that bad. He made me try harder and do better in school. My parents both made sacrifices to make sure we got a good education. What I remember most is him sitting me on the counter and drying my *looonnnggg* hair for me."

When she told me this, it really touched my heart. A few years earlier I had had the privilege of ministering to her in the area of unforgiveness, and I had her start with forgiving me and then we went on to other family members and friends.

That's the way it is supposed to be when we have truly forgiven someone. Only remember the good.

> When we truly forgive someone, we can forget the hurt and only remember the good.

Did he deserve to be forgiven? No, none of us deserves to be forgiven. However, our Father forgives us daily as we fall and miss the mark. Don't you forgive a child when he or she does something wrong? Do you hold it against him or her for life? No. Neither does God. We are His children and slip up so often. He forgives us and welcomes us into His wonderful, loving arms whenever we ask for His forgiveness. The key here is that we have to ask Him to forgive us.

We also have to extend forgiveness whether the other person wants it or not. Unforgiveness doesn't hurt the other person. It hurts us. Bitterness can destroy our bodies. Hate breeds more hate until love is squeezed out of our lives. Fear takes over and isolates us from anyone who could harm us or help us. Again, our choices will make the difference. Do you want to be miserable the rest of your life because of an injustice from years ago? The other person has gone on with his or her life and may even have forgotten what happened. Choose God! Choose to forgive!

Forgive and get on with your life! Will you forget it? A lot of the details will fade. Eventually, you will tell the story as if you were a bystander, a witness to a situation. You will tell the story without the pain or ache you once felt. I know from experience.

## Choose God! Choose to forgive!

How do you do all this? First, ask God to forgive you for your part in the situation. Then, ask Him to forgive the other person. If God can forgive her or her transgressions, you can, too!

If your marriage has ended, take the responsibility for your part in the divorce. Many times the spouse who has been betrayed blames himself or herself. You may feel that you weren't good looking enough or didn't take care of yourself. You might feel you didn't take care of your spouse. You may tend to beat yourself up verbally and mentally.

If you feel responsible in any way for the divorce or causing your spouse to turn to another person, say this prayer out loud:

Father, I take responsibility for my part in this divorce. I know I was not a perfect spouse, but I take that responsibility right now and lay it on Your altar. I release that responsibility and the guilt that comes with it. I release it to You. Father, I thank You for freeing me of this, in Jesus' name.

## Prayer of Forgiveness

Say this prayer:

Father, what (insert the person's name) did to me was sin. It hurt me a lot. It still hurts today. Separate that sin from him/her and put it on the cross of Jesus Christ. And on the day of judgment, I will hold no accusation against him/her. Father, bless him/her.

Father, along with this, take the pain in my heart because of this sin, the emptiness it has left, the bruising, the betrayal. Father, heal me and take all the pain away. I release it to You. Father, allow me to love again. Father, bless them in Jesus' name. Thank You, Jesus.

# Chapter Ten

# Good Counsel

Somewhere along the line, I came to the realization that I was very seriously codependent. Most codependent people are in a dysfunctional relationship with an alcoholic spouse or relative. However, codependency can also relate to many other areas. Drug addiction, obesity, and aberrant lifestyles can factor into the picture.

What is codependency? Simply put, it is when a person's entire life is controlled by another's behavior.

For example, I couldn't make any decisions for myself. I tried to do only what was pleasing to my husband. He made all the decisions for the entire family. My opinion was not important or worthwhile. He presided, provided, and decided. I obeyed and fit into his picture of the perfect family. I was afraid to disagree because he wouldn't like me or want me. He might verbally put me down or, worse yet, abandon me like my birth father had so many years ago.

For many years, I had depended on my mother for approval and love. No one else thought I was worthwhile. Before she married Charles, only my mother would encourage me and try to make me feel good. That dependency was transferred to my spouse after we were married. And then my perspective on that verse in Scripture about "being obedient to your husband" (see 1 Peter 3:1) came into play. I tried to please him in every way I knew how. He was the teacher; I was the student. He taught me proper etiquette. He taught me how to cook. He taught me to decorate the house to his liking. He did everything so well that there was no way I could match his talents. He was so smart and everyone loved him.

When the little doubts would pop into my head, I just hid them. Maybe I ignored them. I didn't want anything to mar the family picture, so I chose not to believe any of the doubts. Christians are supposed to be positive, joyful people. For that reason, I would strive to show only the good, the happy, the beautiful. Smile away the frowns, the tears, the inner pain. Hide behind the mask.

> I believed Christians are supposed to be positive, joyful people and that there was no room for tears and inner pain.

He and his behavior totally controlled my life. I allowed situations to go on even though I questioned his faithfulness. It caused me to tolerate many things that I should have put a stop to years before. For twenty-five years, I believed God to heal the situation because I believed in him. He was a very brilliant man, a very talented man, very gifted, very called.

After the divorce, thoughts tormented me for months and months. *What could I have done differently? Did I do everything I could? What did I do to make him this way? What did I do to turn him away from me? He blamed me, so it must be my fault.* So I blamed myself, too. *After all, he is the smart one. He knows everything. I must have caused all this.*

Then came the thoughts, *I must be ugly. There is something wrong with me. I am ugly. I am fat. I am stupid. No one loves me. Maybe I was wrong. I should have just forgiven him...again.* Then the fear of not having enough finances to survive and put food on the table for the children would start again.

Nobody understands the severity of codependency unless you have been there. It's as bad as a drug addiction that you just can't break. You can't make it without the drug. I knew I couldn't make it in the natural without him. Even the girls knew I couldn't make it in the natural.

If you have ever been addicted to anything—whether it be food, drugs, alcohol, cigarettes—you know the unbelievable desire, the feeling that you just can't get enough. Then imagine going cold turkey. That's the only way I can describe what it is like to be so severely codependent.

I was sick. I was so codependent on him that I believed I could never live financially, spiritually, emotionally, or physically without him. No matter how sick he was, no matter what he was doing, I had been willing to live without any kind of emotional, physical, or mental support from him. I had been willing to go without in every area of my life just to have him there in the house. Next to God, he had been my source of strength and identity.

After he left, I felt like I was totally abandoned without anything sure or true in my life. All my support was gone. I was lost. I didn't know what to do or who to turn to. Yes, I prayed and cried out to God. But even His answers were not filling the emptiness I felt at that time. I had no idea how codependent I was. I don't remember even hearing the word *codependent* until after the divorce. I only know I felt a horrible tearing away, an unbelievable aching in my heart. My whole life just hurt from the giant, empty hole that remained. To look at the empty side of the bed night after night caused more pain than I can fully explain.

No one should ever become that dependent on another person. I chose to ignore situations going on around me. I should have recognized the warning signs. I didn't. I didn't know I should be getting help and advice for this sickness. I shut my eyes and just accepted things as they were. I believed the lies. I was seriously codependent. I was sick.

While I was serving God, ministering healing to hundreds of hurting people, experiencing His power, involved in so many Healing Explosions, a daughter of healing evangelists, and counseling so many others, I was sick. I was blind to my own illness.

Codependency is a sickness, a deception from the enemy to destroy a life. That dependency needed to be on God, not on any human. However, the process of cutting the ties of serious dependency can almost kill the person involved. I speak from personal experience. It takes a lot of work to get back up on your feet.

I could have chosen to remain in my dysfunctional marriage and ignored the infidelity. I could have stayed there for the security of having someone to pay the bills and provide a roof over our heads. Unfortunately, many people do just that. They stay in bondage to lies.

Having to deal with all this, I looked for help. I chose to go to a Spirit-filled, Christian psychotherapist. I explained, "This is the situation…"

He replied, "Plan on another five to seven years to get over this."

"I refuse to give the devil or that man another five to seven years of my life," I told him. "Thank you very much," I said and walked out. Then I added, "I cut those words off. I bind those words in the name of Jesus. They have no power over me. It is not going to take five to seven years to get well."

I knew that God promised to restore the lost years, and I would settle for nothing less.

I would go to the next counselor and he would say, "You do realize it is going to take another five to seven years to recover."

I'd reply, "Thank you very much" and leave. I cut those words off in Jesus' name. I had too much to do to waste another five to seven years.

As I was desperately suffering from all of this, I went to another counselor. He gave me the same textbook answer, "It will take another five to seven years, if ever. In the process of your walking out your healing over that time period, we would like to put you in an institution for at least a month." That's how bad I was. The person I had become needed to be institutionalized. The person I am today doesn't!

Walking out of the counselor's office, I waved my hand over my head and said, "I cut off those words in the name of Jesus, that they will not have power over me. I refuse to let that man rob me of another five to seven years of life. I refuse to give the devil another five to seven years of my life." I knew God had a call on my life and I was not going to spend it in hopelessness.

Although these Spirit-filled counselors were offering help for my problem, I knew that God had promised to restore the lost years, and I would not allow anyone to tell me that He could not restore them in less than seven years. There are good Christian counselors out there, but I ultimately chose to rely on God's knowledge and not the book knowledge the trained counselors were relying on.

As I write this book, it has been six years, but I was 90 percent healed after a year and 100 percent healed after two years, and I have been walking in my healing ever since. God does not operate on man's timeline. God was the answer, and He has done a miraculous healing in all areas of my life.

When negative words were spoken over me, I had to be careful not to accept them. I cut them off in Jesus' name. I had to be very careful whom I spent my time with and the words I listened to. A very close friend actually came up to me and said, "I know you are living in denial. I know you are going to crumble and, when you do, I will be there for you."

I looked her straight in the eye and said, "I am not living in denial. I appreciate the offer, but I am not going to crumble." But I was there for her when she crumbled. I have been a rock for her to help her get through her problems.

I was going through more than just a divorce after twenty-five years, more than just a divorce from a homosexual, more than codependency; there were a lot of other things. During this time, I was also dealing with losing weight. Being overweight has been an ongoing battle for me. I had been about one hundred pounds overweight my whole life. I actually weigh less now than when I was eight years old.

However, after the divorce, I was so sickened by the situation, I continued to lose more weight. It took awhile before I realized why I had been overeating—particularly sweets. My husband hadn't been there for me, so I had tried to fill the emotional void in my life with food, ice cream, and sweets. When I realized why I was emotionally eating, specifically the ice cream, then I was able to stop eating the ice cream.

I had sincerely believed I was doing the best I could do. When I asked God to show me what was hidden and bring the truth to light, I didn't know He would shine His bright spotlight on me. But He did.

What had I done wrong? I lied to myself and to others. I painted a mask on my face to hide my pain. I laughed and smiled like nothing was wrong while I was crying on the inside. I fit into the "perfect pastor's wife" image that he had designed for me. I lied to myself when I should have faced the truth that something was seriously wrong with my marriage. I had nothing on which to base our relationship.

The balance between speaking "positive" words about my deceptive situation and accepting reality was off kilter. I hid the truth from the church, my children, my parents, and myself. But, God knew the truth. Lies had me in bondage, but the truth set me free. However, the pain of understanding and accepting that truth nearly killed me. It did break my heart.

Envy? Yes, I envied other couples who appeared to be so in love. They would cuddle and kiss and hug and laugh. I didn't have that. I wanted that loving relationship I saw in other couples' lives. I knew something was missing.

The most blatant sin I can describe in my life was my putting another person before God. I thought my spouse was the best thing on the earth. I obeyed and believed every word he uttered for so long. There is a fine balance between serving a husband and serving God. God showed me that I had allowed my husband to take first place and that was wrong. I listened to him and took his advice on everything. He was my husband and he was my pastor. He was anointed of God. Shouldn't I be obedient?

> God was the only One who could fill the void in my heart, whether I was married or unmarried.

I was his helpmate but not the kind God had designed me to be. I worked at finding ways to be useful and to fit in within the ministry structure. I'm not sure that he ever needed me to help him because he always seemed to be in control of everything. I tried to be the spouse he wanted me to be, not what God wanted me to be.

I tried to be the mother to my children that they would like and love, not the one God wanted me to be. I loved them and protected them, but he alone controlled the environment and their education. I was the soft touch; he was the strong and strict influence.

I had heard so often, "God first, family second, work last." Somewhere in there, it gets confusing when God is so prominent in all those areas. Our work was to serve God; we were called by God to work in ministry as a family. In my heart, I truly believed we had a great marriage. We had great children, great friends, and the church was our extended "family." But that perfect image came crashing down all around me.

The bomb that went off in my life left a huge gap. We all turn to something to fill our emptiness. We can't stand the void, the empty hole. Some will fill it with smoking, drinking, eating, sex, or spending money excessively.

I had mistakenly looked to my husband to fill the empty area of my heart and life. Suddenly, I knew that God was the only One who could fill that void, whether I was married or not married. Slowly, but surely, God showed me what was happening; indeed, what had happened throughout my life leading up to the period of devastation. Did I feel great overnight? No. But slowly I allowed God to do what He had always wanted. He wanted all of me. I gave Him all of me. He welcomed me, all of me.

I needed God's counsel. I should have spent more time in the past listening to Him. I needed His arms around me to comfort me. I needed Jesus as a brother to love me and to be my very best friend. I needed His Spirit's wisdom and guidance in order to handle all my aches, pains, and hurts. I should have gone to Him instead of my husband or the refrigerator.

My earthly father abandoned me, but God didn't.

My husband deserted me, but God didn't.

My counselor disappointed me, but God didn't.

People have rejected me, but God didn't.

The experts of the world may speak doom and gloom. My Father speaks life.

God loves me.

---

I am His chosen.

---

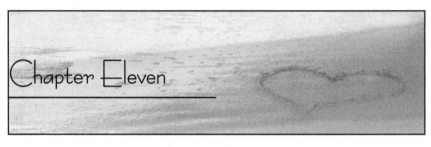

## Chapter Eleven

# Who Am I?

I was forty-six years old. I had been married for twenty-five years. I had raised four children. Suddenly, the nest was empty. I was alone. There was no one home except me and the dogs. I thought, *What do I want for dinner? What do I want to eat?* I didn't even know what I wanted to eat, much less who I was.

In the early days of Mom and Dad's ministry, most people had no idea who I was. Obviously, I was Charles and Frances Hunter's daughter. Thousands of people knew Charles and Frances Hunter. But who was I? Their daughter. Most people did not have a clue what my name was. I was just the Hunters' daughter. Upon occasion, I might be called Miss Hunter. But nobody had any idea who I was. Then, when I got married, I became his wife; when the children came along, I became their mother. Women can take on the identity of a wife or mother. Men can take on the identity that comes from their jobs or professions.

Not that I resented that, by any means, but I didn't know who I was. I was Charles and Frances Hunter's daughter. I was the pastor's wife. I was the girls' mother. I was the employee of the car company. I defined myself by the roles I filled, not by who I was. I had one of the lowest self-esteems that you could ever fathom in this world. It was so low, I essentially had none.

There was no self about me, about who I was or what I wanted to do, or what I wanted to be. Yes, I had wanted to be a good pastor's wife. I wanted to be a good mother. I wanted to be a good daughter. And I was good at all of them.

In the process of growing up, I had been told that I was retarded. I was told I was so dumb I would never accomplish anything. I was told I would always be morbidly obese. I was told I would never accomplish anything because I was so dumb, so stupid, so ugly, and a variety of other things. We tend to take on the attributes people have spoken over us, whether they are true or not.

I remember when everyone listened to messages by Kenneth Hagin or Kenneth Copeland. Then they would get in the pulpit and preach like Kenneth Hagin or Kenneth Copeland. They would read notes from those messages. We would call them "Haginites" or "Copelandites." The preachers didn't know who they were so they copied others.

We all have mentors or other people we want to be like, but we shouldn't idolize them to the point that we try to imitate everything about them. Through the years, especially as my parents grew older, people would tell me I needed to start acting more like my mother—to practice the way she speaks, to practice her mannerisms, "the way your mom does this, the way your mom does that."

I would listen and say, "Thank you very much." Then I would start conforming to what people expected of me. I thought, *Okay, well, I could probably go like this or like this and be a little more like Mom.* And I would attempt to copy her mannerisms.

God would rebuke me, "Do you want to do it her way or My way?"

"Excuse me, Father; I want to do things Your way!"

I can't tell you how many people told me that I am a Frances Hunter. No! No disrespect to her, but God said, "One Frances Hunter is enough! If I wanted another one, I would have made two." And He continued, "One Joan Hunter is enough. I'm not making more than one." Obviously, there are some similarities because she is my mother, but I am not a Frances Hunter. God doesn't want me to be a Frances Hunter. God has custom-made each of us. We are all different. Even the hairs on our heads are numbered and our fingerprints are unique.

> God has custom-made each of us. Even the hairs on our heads are numbered and our fingerprints are unique.

We need to take on the attributes of God.

God gave me this Scripture. It is from Joshua 24:15. *"Choose you this day whom ye will serve;...but as for me and my house, we will serve the LORD"* (KJV). Joshua did not say, "I will serve my past or others' expectations for me."

I choose to serve the Lord. If I had chosen to serve my past, I would have made an idol of it.

I don't want to serve the past. I don't want to be that list of negative attributes that people made for me. I don't want to be that person "who could never do anything, so why even try?" It was a death wish that had been spoken over me in years gone by. So many times I reverted back to thinking, *Oh, you are right. I will never accomplish anything. No wonder I made a mistake. I am proving them right again.* I can't remember how many times I have said that about myself. *You are right. I can't do anything right.*

But that particular Scripture is *"Choose you this day."* Due to the amount of put-downs I experienced through the years, upon a very rare occasion, the thoughts come back. Very, very rarely do they come back now, compared to the days when they would come back every five minutes to beat me down.

But when I gave it to the Lord, I put it all on His altar, all the verbal abuse that I had received while growing up from my peers, various relatives, and others. With all the negativism, the constant put-downs that I received, it was very difficult to believe I could do anything right. I was told, "You can't clean the house worth anything," so I didn't even try, and I proved them right.

One day, I was praying and asking God about different situations in my life. First, I was trying to figure out who I was. Second, at the time, I was trying to decide what I wanted for dinner. As simple as that was, I really didn't have any idea what Joan wanted to eat.

Then I realized that I was going to have to make some other decisions. How did I want to wear my hair? I had never had that choice before. Instead of being asked to keep it long, I could cut my hair and wear it short. I could actually make my own decision how I wanted to style my hair. It was a very liberating experience.

I had been bound by what other people had spoken over me. It didn't make any difference if my hair was long or short. I had the freedom to cut my hair. I got very excited and cut my hair very short. And I loved it.

I made some other changes in my life, also. Through the years, people have told me my best feature is my eyes. Well, when you are morbidly obese and look like a balloon, at least you can have good-looking eyes. I lost weight, and then I had laser surgery done so I could get rid of those big, thick glasses.

Through the years, the only positive comment ever spoken over me about my personal appearance was about my eyes. So I spent time doing my makeup and accentuating my eyes. I realized I had something beautiful that I needed to highlight. Yes, I do have pretty eyes. I discovered that I had inward beauty and outward beauty, and it all was a gift from God. I just helped it a little.

Do I look different now than I did? Yes, I did have an overhaul in the natural with my hair and a variety of other things. I can go shopping wearing blue jeans. But God has totally revolutionized me, changed me inside and out. While shopping in a store, my girls would call out, "Mom, where are you?" My own children had a hard time recognizing me because God had done so much for me.

A few years ago, I went to my parents' condo to prepare for a television interview. Using my key, I walked in and surprised them. My dad looked at me and said, "Where's my daughter? What have you done with her?" *What a compliment!*

Before the physical transformation, I had to think about who I was. I started saying, "Well, I think I'm beautiful."

I knew I couldn't stop there. I had to say, "I know I am beautiful." It was very, very difficult to say. I remember the first time I said it. It was as if a boulder got stuck in my throat because I had so often been told otherwise. I had to make a list of who I am, who God wants me to be, as well as many other positive attributes about myself. I posted the list on my mirror where I could see and read them every day. They were a reminder to me.

Anybody who has seen me as a mother, as a wife, as a minister, knows that I am loving. I am merciful. I am a giver. I am sincere. I am a servant. I am a faithful friend. And I am beautiful. And the mirror is not big enough for me to include everything on the list. I had to do whatever I could to change what I had in my heart and mind to what God had waiting for me. I want you to change your thinking about who you are, too.

> I am merciful. I am a giver. I am a servant. I am a faithful friend. And I am beautiful.

You may say, "I'm too busy to think about myself."

I believe God wants us to think about ourselves sometimes. How am I eating? Am I eating properly? Am I getting enough rest? Am I getting enough exercise? Am I reading the Bible enough? Am I feeding myself spiritually? I had to develop who I was meant to be. Because I went through that process, when I minister to someone else, I can now minister as a whole person.

Now I know who I am. I know not only who I am but that I am loving, I am a giver, I am anointed, and I am called. I am gifted. I know that. I know who I am in Christ. Now I know who I am!

Start a list to put on your mirror. Add positive attributes whenever you think of one and watch it grow!

I was looking at some pictures one day. One of the pictures showed me at age twenty-six. When you look at any picture, you usually look at the eyes because the eyes are the windows of the soul. When you look at this particular picture, you see a young woman who is lost and didn't know who she was. She knew who she was in Christ, but otherwise didn't know who she was. She continued to eat to fill the void in her life.

I have another picture of the same person years later. The woman in the second picture knows who she is. Not just someone who knows who she is in Christ, but someone who knows who she is. When the photographer took this picture of me, he said, "There is something about your eyes. During my twenty-one years' experience in the photography business, I have never seen eyes like yours. They sparkle like they are under movie spotlights."

But these are the eyes of the same person in both photographs. However, today these are the eyes of somebody who knows who she is. Somebody who sparkles with the love of Jesus Christ in her heart; somebody who knows that God has called her, God has separated her out, and God has protected her through the years. Somebody who knows she is beautiful. Not that *I think* that I am beautiful. This is not an ego thing. You need to know you are beautiful inside and out.

I remember ministering to a man who had no clue how to love his wife. His comment was, "How can I love my wife if I don't even love myself?"

How can you love your spouse if you don't even love yourself? How can you love other people that you minister to if you don't love yourself? If you don't know who you are, you are not ministering from the standpoint of who they can be.

I can minister night after night, day after day, knowing that God has called me and anointed me. Nobody can ever take that from me. Not height or depth, not principalities or powers. Nothing can ever take that fact away from me. (See Romans 8:38.)

I can now minister with confidence because I know who I am.

When I was traveling with Mom and Dad in the early years, I had such low self-esteem that I knew I could not do anything. I felt I was worthless. After all, I was only Charles and Frances Hunter's daughter. If you'd had an opportunity to have my mom, my dad, or me minister to you twenty or thirty years ago, who would you have gone to?

I would hide behind the biggest, blackest curtain. Mom would find me every time and force me to shake hands with the people. They could care less to shake hands with me. But it would get me out from behind the curtain.

Many people are hiding behind the curtain. Some are hiding from the world. There are physical attitudes that show people are hiding. When you are experienced enough, you can recognize these things. They will hide their faces, hide their mouths, or hide their eyes.

I don't have to hide my eyes anymore. My eyes are clean. I have the sparkle of Jesus Christ in my eyes. I now can minister to a congregation, really to anybody. I minister everywhere—in grocery stores, in malls, in airports, in airplanes. Everywhere I go, I minister to people.

I don't have a fear of being rejected. Jesus took rejection on the cross so I don't have to suffer rejection. He took the pain on the cross so I don't have to suffer pain. He knew who He was, and He wants to impart to us who we are. It is very crucial that we know that.

I had believed a lie all those years. I was not retarded. I don't have a genius IQ. But that's okay. My mother and my brother do, and they can have them. God gives me the wisdom I need.

> I believed lies about myself, but God healed my heart and showed me who I am in Him.

I was told that I would be morbidly obese my whole life, so why even try to diet? I had believed a lie.

Between the ages of three and six, I was molested by an uncle. I praise God that He has healed my heart and redeemed me from that experience. But for a very long time, in the case of being molested, I had believed a lie. It was *not* my fault.

I could go on and on and on about many instances where I had to go back and say, "I believed a lie about myself." Say this aloud regarding anything that has been spoken over you or done to you: "I believed a lie. I believed a lie about myself! I am not _____! I have believed a lie! I am _____!"

God wants to use me. Does He want to use me the same way as my parents? No. Who am I to ever compare myself with Charles and Frances Hunter? I am not supposed to compare myself with Charles and Frances Hunter. I thank God that they are my mom and dad. But I will never be them.

I want to be the best *me* that I can be. I want to be on a constant upward stride to better myself. Am I perfect? No, but that's my goal. I want to be a better person and minister of God than I have ever been before. I want my relationship with the Lord to grow every day. I want to constantly improve my relationship with Him. I want to minister to others with more of His anointing. And every day I want to improve my relationship with myself.

If you were to choose one person to spend the rest of your life with, would you choose yourself? Many people say no.

Some time ago, I was on the way to New York as a keynote speaker at a big convention. I made it. My CDs and DVDs made it. My clothes didn't make it. My makeup didn't make it. My jewelry didn't make it. My shoes didn't make it. My toothbrush didn't make it. Several other things didn't make it. It was a disconcerting situation.

A very formal affair was scheduled for Sunday night, and I didn't have my clothes. The only shops available were discount stores. I wasn't exactly crushed, but it was a very humbling experience. I like pretty clothes, but they are not my god.

I got up to minister during that conference and the anointing was very strong. I didn't feel very comfortable in the clothes I was in because I had planned on wearing my pretty yellow suit with rhinestones. Instead, I had on an out-fit that wasn't even business casual. I didn't have the right shoes. I didn't have the right jewelry. I am very thematic and everything needs to match. If not, I feel like I am missing a foot. That's just my personality type. If you are that way, you will understand. If you're not, you may think I'm strange.

Nice clothes make me feel good. I like flowers. I like smelling good. I like looking good. I don't even do yard work without my makeup on. The more I want to feel my best, the more I make myself look better.

There were many things that I lost, like my daily devotional Bible that I had had for thirty years. My jewelry was lost—the only time I didn't wear my rings. I bought another Bible, and I knew God would restore my rings. The airlines called weeks later to inform me they had closed my case—there was no hope of finding my suitcase. Shortly afterward, I was blessed with jewelry and new clothes.

Nothing happens without a reason. I know that the healing of the heart ministry that I have is not for my glory. It is for God's glory, for God to use what happened to me as He sets people free around the world.

I prayed about it. And I was asked to think why my suitcase is lost. God showed me a lot of reasons why it was lost. There were a few things that I always had on my body that were in that suitcase. There is a specific reason why they are gone.

One thing God showed me is very important. He showed me that my clothes do not make me beautiful. Sometimes I feel good in my pretty, feminine blue outfit. I feel pretty when I am wearing it. But if I put on an old pair of jeans, I am still beautiful. It was a great realization when God showed me I was beautiful with or without my yellow suit or my turquoise pantsuit, which was my earthly dad's favorite.

People tell me I look younger than I did ten years ago. I have a good friend whom I went to school with some thirty years ago. I ran into him some time ago and said, "Hi!" and gave him a great big hug.

He looked at me rather strangely, and I could imagine him thinking, *Who's this person hugging me?*

"It's Joan."

He said, "My Joan?"

I answered, "Yes!"

And then he said, "Ooh!" and hugged me. I'm sure that the differences in my appearance had an effect on his reaction, as well as the amount of time since we had seen each other. But the change that happened on the inside showed up on my face. It definitely showed up as a change in my eyes. The power in my voice has changed, too. I know who I am!

> I love ministering and seeing people change. The light of Jesus Christ is shining through their eyes.

I love ministering and seeing the change in people's eyes. Their eyes just light up, and they sparkle. The light of Jesus Christ is shining through their eyes. During those times, I realize even more the change in my appearance was because of Him. I remember the feeling of freedom, of peace, of joy when I allowed Him to heal my heart and mind. And I cry with those I minister to as they change before my eyes.

There have been many words spoken over me through the years. Some good. The majority of them not so good.

As I have ministered to people, I have said, "Words have been spoken over you." God will reveal to me who has been the hardest on that person. And it is always themselves. I deal with my own self put-downs more than everybody else's put together.

Negative words are piercing and penetrating, with long-lasting effects.

A major airline had one of the lowest customer service ratings there ever was and they were going to file bankruptcy. A new president went around telling the employees what a good job they were doing. Now, their customer service satisfaction ratings are one of the top in the nation because of affirmation, because of positive words spoken over the employees.

Employers need to speak positive words over their employees. Parents need to speak positive words over their children. Marriage partners need to speak positive words over their spouses. We all need to speak good things over others.

Yes, some of those words need to be confessions by faith, such as "My children are taught of the Lord and *great is their peace*, in the name of Jesus. My children are taught of the Lord, and when they are old, they will not depart from it, and great is their peace." (See Isaiah 54:13.)

I am seeing those words manifested more and more every day. I confess those Scriptures over my children, not only in the privacy of my room, but also over the telephone when I talk to them. They are scattered all over the nation now, but I remind them that they are highly favored of the Lord. I speak positive things over my children because it makes them want to strive to do better. It encourages them to do more, not for me, but for themselves.

Do you know the favor you walk in, not only because of yourself, but also because of your parents and grandparents?

*But the mercy of the LORD is from everlasting to everlasting on those who fear Him, and His righteousness to children's children.*　　　(Psalm 103:17)

*His descendants will be mighty on earth; the generation of the upright will be blessed.*　　　(Psalm 112:2)

*And His mercy is on those who fear Him from generation to generation.*　　　(Luke 1:50)

Your parents and grandparents have had a definite effect on your life. Their respect for God determined God's respect and blessings on your life. I thank God I have wonderful Christian parents who have been an inspiration through the years. What I do now for God will have an effect on my children. Believe me when I say that I want all His blessings to shower over my beautiful children and grandchildren!

Think positive and speak positive to yourself and your children.

Look into the mirror. Whether you believe you are beautiful or not, you need to say, "I am beautiful. I am beautiful." I have said it so much that I know I am beautiful.

Wherever I go to minister, people tell me, "You are so beautiful."

I say, "Thank you, thank you, thank you. I appreciate that." But it doesn't mean anything unless I know it in my heart. When I used to look in the mirror, I never saw what they saw. But now I do.

I wrote down the things that I am. I add to the list on a daily basis. I want to be more Godlike. God is a lover. God never lies. He is sincere. He is a friend. God is *my* friend. God is a servant. He will do for me whatever I need and what is best for me. He longs to make sure that everything is perfect for me. And I need to be more like God and take on His nature.

God is a lover!
God never lies!
He is my friend!
And I am His!

And I want to know who I am. Instead of being a "Haginite" or "Copelandite," I want to be a Jesus-ite. I want to be more Godlike.

I have always wanted to see and experience the love of God. We are the only representatives that Jesus has on this earth. And we need to take on His nature. But the only way I can do that is by allowing God to flow through me to others.

I want to be who God wants me to be.

I am full of grace…like God.

I am merciful…like God.

I am patient…like God.

I am a giver…like God.

I am loving…like God.

I am understanding…like God.

I am beautiful…like God.

# Chapter Twelve

# Pitfalls and Deceptions: Will Anyone Ever Love Me?

When any relationship changes or ends, emotions and feelings are always affected. Whether it be a job change, relocation, serious illness, death, or divorce, stress increases. Mental, emotional, and physical effects can be anything from seriously positive to seriously negative or a combination of both. Our lives are molded and shaped by these experiences. We call it life. Nothing is all positive or all negative. How we handle these situations becomes our choice.

For instance, the world's view of newlyweds is a picture of blissful happiness. Anyone who is or has been married knows this is not 100 percent true. Moving to and setting up a new home; leaving parents and family; adjusting to another's habits, desires, and dreams twenty-four hours a day instead of a few hours during a date; giving up privacy; getting along with in-laws—the list goes on and on. Even the words of some wedding vows promise both positive and negative: sickness and health, richer or poorer.

Parents may be glad for their children to move out, to go to school, or to start their own lives; however, most then experience feelings of loneliness and the loss of the children's presence in their everyday lives. Positive and negative.

A change of jobs may bring in more money or prestige; however, it may mean relocation to another city with a complete change of support system, with new friends, neighbors, and/or church. Positive and negative.

Whether a husband/wife relationship is wonderful, loving, and healthy; or abusive, unpleasant, and dangerous, the separation will have serious effects. Positive and negative.

Was I glad to be out of this relationship? No. Any relationship was better than none. I had thought everything would work out for the best. I was always an optimist. I was so sure I could fix the problem.

> No experience in life is completely negative or completely positive. How we respond is our choice.

Was I embarrassed? Yes. Even though he was the guilty one, he wasn't embarrassed. He went on with his life as if everything was fine. I chose to take on his embarrassment and felt I was responsible. Was I responsible? Partially, because I ignored the warning signs of improper behavior that I should have addressed years ago. I swallowed one insult, then two, then three, and so on. just like I ignored the first symptom of a problem, then the second, and all the rest.

After living with my spouse for twenty-five years, one would think I knew him very well. I shared everything with him. Why would I suspect that he didn't share things with me? I gave my all to him. Why didn't he do the same?

Trust was broken. Betrayal blared. Rejection laughed hysterically. Desertion trampled over me. Fear overwhelmed me. The old feelings of being unlovable and a failure inundated my mind.

Many people, both men and women, become so emotionally starved that they go the opposite direction and want to be overwhelmed with affection and respect. There has to be a balance.

For instance, one woman shared some details about her experience after a divorce. A man came along and offered her the world—affection, adoration, and tender loving care—a man who was also in the ministry, just as she was, willing to protect her and take care of her. He was her dream come true, her knight in shining armor, God's answer to her prayer.

She was very hungry for affection following her difficult and painful divorce. Everything that the ex-husband was, the new person wasn't. Everything the ex-husband wasn't, the new man was. After several months, the relationship changed. Some of his other attributes started to surface. He had a seductive spirit. He knew what to say to get his way.

However, this time she started to back off and resist accepting some of his behavior. Lies, lack of responsibility, and desertion reared their ugly heads. The relationship ended. Pain, frustration, anger, rejection followed...again. She seriously doubted she could ever trust a man again.

Because of hurt, pain, and fear, we tend to build walls. In order to avoid the pain of betrayal and hurt, we choose not to trust again. This is not a good or realistic situation, but it is one that frequently occurs after such a bad experience.

After being hurt, abused, or misused, many withdraw and avoid any kind of relationship with another person.

In a situation like mine, it is common to wonder if everyone I trusted or met was hiding a secret. This fear becomes a phobia of repeating the same kind of relationship. It is good to be cautious for a time, in many cases, since it seemed inconceivable that it would happen in the first place. I never believed in divorce. I still don't. But I was forced to get divorced from him to save my life.

Many codependent personalities tend to go back into the same type of relationship to continue to "fix" the problems the next person exhibits. Believing the empty promises of the next partner can draw the vulnerable, hurting person into another trap of codependency, into another abusive situation. Women often look for men who are like their fathers. Looking for positive qualities sounds ideal; however, often the similarities between father and husband also include the negative.

For example, Sela's father was an alcoholic. She married a man who was an alcoholic. They were divorced, and she was remarried to another alcoholic. She endured physical abuse throughout every relationship. This repetitive behavior is usually tied to a generational curse, and it needed to be broken or it would have continued through to Sela's children.

A generational curse is something that is passed down from generation to generation, such as cancer, diabetes, or high blood pressure. But generational curses aren't just medical or genetic. They can also be things like anger, emotional problems, child abuse, and spousal abuse. These need to be broken so they are not passed down to future generations.

Deception, lies, and controlling manipulation are all forms of witchcraft. Witchcraft isn't just spells and black cats, but anything a person uses to control or manipulate another. They are destructive weapons of the enemy. They are similar to cancer of the brain. Starting small with one little seed, soon they uncontrollably replicate and replace truth and reason. These people are so good at what they do that everyone around them is totally deceived as if they were brainwashed. They can promise the world and fool their victims—at least, for awhile. They can be found attending many Christian functions and can draw the unsuspecting, trusting Christian into their web of deception.

> Man was created for relationship—with God and with other people. But true happiness only comes from God.

Deception, alcohol, and abuse—all indicate a seductive spirit! They entice a person into doing something they normally wouldn't choose to do! *Seduction* normally refers to sexual intimacy; however, it can be applied to many other areas of life, also.

There is an old adage that a man completes a woman or vice versa. This would falsely indicate that true fulfillment can only be found with a person of the opposite sex, that there has to be two to be happy, two to be truly one.

Indeed, man was created for relationship. In man's eyes, that relationship is expected to involve another human being. And yes, we do need one another. We need to interact and love and be with other people. However, we may often interpret the loneliness we feel as a need for another person when we actually should be looking elsewhere. Looking for fulfillment from man, and true happiness from a spouse or relationship, will not fill the void we feel within our hearts.

Jesus is the only One who can fill the void. We have to look to God, Jesus, and the Holy Spirit for the answer to our every need, including the loneliness, the void. Love from Him fulfills all our needs.

After you have been hurt, you may ask, What about a future relationship? How can I love again? How can I trust again?

If you sincerely want to get married, God will bless you with someone. However, there are some precautions I want to share with you at this point. Just because the enemy has destroyed a marriage doesn't mean he will leave you alone from then on. The more God has for you in your future, the harder the enemy will fight for your total destruction. I do speak from experience on that point.

There are many pitfalls along the way to total recovery. How you choose to react to them is the key to your success or failure.

When you are plagued with loneliness and believe no one wants you anymore, there is always the temptation to accept any and every invitation you receive without discrimination. You may find yourself in precarious situations without the ability to extricate yourself safely. After being discarded by a spouse, it is hard to regain confidence that you are still desirable and worthwhile. There is always that temptation to sleep around to prove you are still wanted by another.

You may think you were the best thing that ever happened to your spouse and, in reality, you probably were. You tried to help your spouse in every possible area, but he or she didn't appreciate you. You were a giver; your spouse was a taker. Even though you know you did your best, after the fact, you still doubt and wonder. It is difficult to realize the other person's contribution to the problem; it's not all your fault. If you ask God, He will show you the underlying problem. You may not like it; however, He will show you if you are willing to listen.

Why should you ask? You need to prepare yourself and make some changes before entering into another relationship. You may carry some of the same baggage into marriage the next time.

It is difficult to ignore the doubts, but you must. The enemy will feed you lies, such as "Your next mate will desert you!" "He is going to have an affair and lie about it," "He is going to start drinking and abuse you," or "He is gay!" You have to deal with the fear that can paralyze you and the mistrust that can destroy your next relationship.

What do you do in the valley? Go back to the list in chapter five, start with number one, and keep going down the list. You may have to repeat these steps daily, weekly, or monthly. Remember, challenges will come. Your response to them will determine the outcome. We are responsible only for our own response. How someone else responds to the situation is his or her responsibility. We can't *fix* someone else. Only God can! Go back to number one and continue repeating those steps as often as necessary. They will help you focus on God because He is the answer!

Unfortunately, traumatic destruction of families affects more than the man and woman involved. Like the impact of a pebble that drops in the middle of a serene pond of water, the ripples continue to rush outward. The bomb that went off in my home did the same. I still get feedback from friends on their reactions and feelings about the situation.

You may not have experienced these situations yourself, but almost everyone has met or knows someone who has suffered some traumatic event. Whether divorce, homosexuality, abuse, alcohol, or death, please follow up with the spouse, the victim of the situation. Let them know you are praying for them. You don't need to know the details. Let them share when and if they choose to do so. Above all, don't repeat things they share with you in confidence. It is no one else's business. Let them know you care even if you have no answers. Everyone is in shock. No one knows what to do or say. Most people do nothing, which actually leaves the victim high and dry—and very alone and scared.

> I once thought I was the only one with these problems. The truth has set me free, and now I can help others.

Since I have shared my testimony around the world over the past few years, others have come to me to say, "The same thing happened to me! I'm so glad to know I am not the only one who has suffered with this problem!"

I once thought I was the only one with these problems, also. The truth has set me free. Now I can help others get free, as well. We are not in this battle by ourselves. We have to hold each other up—sometimes physically, occasionally mentally, often emotionally, but most definitely spiritually.

We all know the platitudes, "You're better off without him!" "Be glad you don't have to deal with him anymore," "Time heals all wounds." In the middle of the disaster zone, such statements sound fine, but actually don't help much.

People need others who will stand with them and support them. If they are lonely, just be there! If they are hungry, feed them! If they need to talk, let them. If they need to cry, let them. If they want prayer, pray. The one thing everyone needs is love, God's love. And we, as God's servants, must allow His love to flow through us to the ones who are hurting. Be willing to show His love!

I know the thrill of freedom. My sincere desire is that everyone who reads this book will find the same freedom.

I love being the vessel to bring freedom to others. You will, too!

Don't plan on hiding your experiences! Don't let the enemy win! Share what has happened. Tell others how you have overcome and won the battle! Tell others that God set you free! Every time you share your testimony, you are stomping on the devil's head in victory!

## Thank You, Jesus!

# I Am Not Alone

ince sharing my testimony, many people have felt led to share their experiences with me. I have included several stories here. Of course, their names have been changed to preserve their privacy. Yes, these are the testimonies of their battles; however, more importantly, these stories proclaim their victories!

Here are just a few of the hundreds of thousands who have gone through similar situations as mine. I wanted to share them with you. They all bring a different aspect to His healing power and His grace. These testimonies are from healed people. Betrayal is betrayal, whether it comes in the form of same-sex or heterosexual affairs. The good news is that God can heal them all!

Every one of the stories shared in this chapter is headed toward a happy ending. Each person turned to God and found His healing touch through His Word, His Christian counselors, and His pastors. They are all living healthy and whole lives, free from unforgiveness, pain, feelings of rejection, and betrayal. They all want to give God the glory for taking them through this time in their lives. For without Him, none of us would have made it through. Thank You, Jesus.

A friend of mine is a doctor. She and her husband, B.K., were both active in their church and had been in church leadership for many years. After forty-eight years of marriage, B.K.'s father admitted he was homosexual and wanted a divorce. His mother was devastated. B.K. was so upset by this revelation that he started sleeping around indiscriminately, including with prostitutes, to prove to himself and others that he wasn't gay. His reaction destroyed his relationship with his wife, his relationship with the church, and his relationship with his children. They were divorced, and all are continuing to try to survive and resume some semblance of normal life.

S.Z. had a spouse who was an active pedophile as well as gay. When their son discovered what his father was doing, he reported him to the authorities. The father was arrested and imprisoned. Even though the son did the right thing, he still has to deal with the guilt of turning against his father. The family is destroyed.

> Every one of these stories had a happy ending when God took control of the situation.

D.B. and her spouse were anointed praise and worship leaders until her spouse was caught having an affair with a man in their church. Of course, a divorce followed. Their son adjusted poorly to the family breakup. As a teenager, he unsuccessfully tried to commit suicide. His suicide note explained he would rather be dead than have a father who is homosexual. After medical treatment, he suddenly developed epileptic seizures now attributed to a chemical imbalance caused by his attempt to end his pain and suffering.

D.B.'s happy ending includes remarriage to a wonderful, godly husband. The son is in counseling.

B.J.'s husband broke up their family for his homosexual lifestyle. She described him as selfish; he never considered the consequences of his actions. "He knew I would never divorce him so he kept doing it. He was so deceived. He didn't think it was wrong. He never thought about what it would do to the children. He was surprised to find they were affected at all. They wonder why he kept it up for so long. If he was so miserable, why didn't he just leave? The family provided him with something that he never had. He liked being with the family, belonging to a family, but preferred being with other men."

W.T. finally learned to accept her father's homosexuality but can't handle the lies. He lied before and is still lying. She estimates only one out of thirty statements may possibly be true. Behind all the lies, he still claims to love W.T. and the other siblings. Since their mother isn't there anymore to act as a buffer, the grown children have to adjust and deal with the father's deception on their own. They have to choose their own path to recovery.

Another Christian couple were pastors of a local church. In this case, the wife had an affair with another woman. Because of denominational laws, she had to leave the city. She and her partner are now pastoring in another city. The husband, who was the senior pastor, has disappeared. No one knows where he is. The church members are still trying to recover.

Another man had been a pastor for over thirty years. On his deathbed, he finally confessed to his spouse that he was homosexual and had had affairs the entire forty-eight years of their marriage. Deception, lies, and sin—with far-reaching effects!

## Sara's Story

My first clue that something was deeply, terribly wrong was when my eighteen-year-old son broke down in the middle of a conversation. His voice jumped an octave, and through held-back tears he said, "Mom, you don't understand, he's done things!"

My heart and stomach flipped, and my body turned cold in an instant. I didn't know yet what the problem was, but I knew it was serious. I don't know why, but my immediate thought was that my husband had touched our son inappropriately. I pressed him for information, but he wouldn't say more. I let the matter rest and, after my spouse left for work, I went to my son's room, sat on his bed, and waited for him to talk.

That's when I learned the truth about my husband of twenty-four years. My son had found child pornography on his computer and called the police. A criminal investigation had been underway for some time as the police had been doing background work on my husband, pillar in the community, active church member, husband and father.

The rest of the day was a blur. Now that I knew, the police brought me into the investigation. The humiliation of having the sheriff walk the length of my office building in search of me was devastating. I thought I wouldn't be able to live it down, but it was just the beginning of the humiliation and abuse I would suffer for his actions.

I spent three weeks caring for his needs, cooking, cleaning, kissing him good-bye each day as if nothing was wrong. All the while, my heart was screaming at him to wake up, fall on his knees, and repent before it was too late. I now have a new insight into what praying without ceasing means.

Several weeks later, my son called and told me to come home. The sheriff had just served a search warrant at the house. I arrived at home to find my driveway packed with nine police cars! My front door was standing open, and a sheriff was at the door guarding it. Inside, the house was swarming with officers wearing little plastic gloves, taking photos, and bagging evidence. I sank onto the couch next to my son and watched as if I were sitting in the middle of a theater production. It couldn't possibly be happening to my family.

> I now have a new insight into what praying without ceasing means.

The lead investigator later pulled me aside to tell me that they had found child porn on the computer. There were papers to sign and then they packed up to leave. I stood at the door and said good-bye to each, my mother's training on manners coming to serve while I was in shock. My son and I went to the hardware store and bought new locks, changing them before calling him or confronting him at work.

Later, after everyone had gone to bed, I stood silent vigil at the front door; I imagined that behind the drawn shades and curtains of every neighbor was at least one set of eyes watching my house, their phones ringing as gossip spread like wildfire throughout the community.

A few days later, the sheriff came to my office again. He reported that they had found the child porn—in fact, it was the largest collection ever uncovered. There was so much that it was almost beyond their ability to prosecute. I didn't know how much more I could handle. My husband was calling me every few minutes, begging to come home, promising to change, planning to get help, pleading, growing angry, resorting to tears; I was emotionally spent as I rode the roller coaster of emotions.

As the sheriff sat across from my desk that day, he said one other thing before he left. "There were over 4400 images on the hard drive and approximately one hundred disks of images on the desk, as well. Ma'am, not all the images were of children. About half were children and the rest were men and young boys. There were only a few pictures of women." He spoke softly, but the words drove into my spirit as if he had used his gun.

That was two days of my life a year and a half ago. I never dreamed my life would turn out like this, never dreamed the man I had married was leading a double life. I never had a clue that he was gay. Perhaps I was naïve; perhaps I was just too wrapped up in life in general. I knew he wasn't happy, yet he truly hadn't been happy most of our marriage. He had no interest in sex and, after the last round of counseling had not helped, I made a decision. If he was injured in a car accident and couldn't make love to me, I wouldn't divorce him. I loved him, so I made a decision to let go of my expectations regarding that part of our marriage and settled into a lackluster marriage that seemed to work everywhere but the bedroom. I had no idea that the rug was about to be pulled out from under my world.

This was the third breakup I had had with my husband; each time we had put things back together. I believe the Lord allowed me to experience the total breadth of emotions during these three breakups. The first time, I was absolutely and totally devastated. I couldn't eat, couldn't sleep. The second, I was so angry at him and God that I was out of control.

This time I was washed in relief. I know it sounds insane, but I spent so many years battling the unknown. I never knew whether he was having a bad day. I spent my life walking on eggshells to avoid the anger, wrath, and abuse.

I knew there was no patching this time. This time I knew the real reason behind all our problems. They say the truth shall set you free, and that is exactly what it did for me. I was relieved. It is the only word that describes how I feel. My worth as a wife and sexual partner had been painfully stripped away a layer at a time over the years. I had long since given up my ideas of more children and a passionate, intimate relationship with my husband. I had settled for the sake of the marriage. I had spent years blaming myself, losing my self-esteem, my self-worth, allowing an existence of nothingness to stand for a marriage instead of leaving for my health and the health of my son. How could I know the real truth that lay at the bottom of our marriage, hidden under lies, deception, abuse, and control?

I've long since given up trying to understand. I've accepted the fact that he lied to me from our first date. His phone confession to having a homosexual encounter in high school means that even before we had dated, the sin was there. He admitted to being confused. He admitted to being with a man since our last round of counseling. That was enough for me. There was no turning back.

I know many women resist leaving marriage for fear of not being able to cope—God is the one who copes; you just walk in His footsteps.

Many women are afraid that no one will love them again. Your husband doesn't love you and hasn't ever really, truly, loved you. Only Jesus loves you, wholly, completely, and unconditionally.

Some women are afraid they will be lonely. Truthfully, aren't you lonely now? I have not suffered one day or night of loneliness since this has happened. I was lonely in the marriage, but I am not lonely now—Jesus is my constant companion.

> I am not lonely now. Jesus is my constant companion.

Many women are afraid they won't be able to afford to leave their husband and his income. Remember, Jesus is your sole provider. He has provided for all my needs, right down to, "Lord, I don't have a car, and I can't afford one." Within one week, the Lord provided me with a car, completely paid for. All I had to do was purchase the new tags!

My walk with the Lord is much closer and deeper than it was before this happened. He has been my constant companion, provider, and protector. Even when I don't understand the whys, I have learned to trust Him more deeply to be in charge of my life. I know that God has great plans for me and intends to use me mightily for His glory through this. I wait with joyful anticipation of what the future holds.

# Kay's Story

As I look back on my life, I am finally free to discuss the incredible feelings of both hurt and healing after being married to a gay man. I have been told I am a very attractive woman in the corporate world with a very successful track record. But until knowing Christ and being set free, I felt like a captive—an unattractive woman who seemed to be a total failure, continually trying to gain approval, especially in relationships.

We married right out of high school because that is what was done forty years ago. I had only dated my husband for six months before the wedding, with no knowledge of the details I am about to share. At the time, I also had a stepfather who disliked me intensely (another relationship of rejection), so getting married seemed like a great way of escape. Little did I know that I was escaping one prison and entering another.

At first, I was so excited to be married and thought time would make everything better. As time went on, the problems started. It became evident that I had made a horrible mistake. I had married a gay man.

He wanted to have a baby right away. Knowing what I know now, a baby was a way of making him seem okay and somewhat normal. I refused to start off with a baby since I was just learning to be a wife myself. Four years later, we had a beautiful daughter, and I thought she would make things better. After all, now we looked like the all-American family with a beautiful child.

Things appeared to be normal. Our total focus was on our daughter, as is normal with most new parents. However, his controlling behavior, which had become evident to me, increased even more. I thought perhaps I was just a bad mother. I tried to learn to be a better mom, a better wife. Nothing seemed to please the man I married. Everything was "my fault" that things were not working.

As we continued, things became worse. I had opened a very successful boutique. I focused on my work since there seemed to be no way to make my marriage a success. The community recognized my success. Even newspapers were publishing articles about my successful business. However, my husband could never give me any compliment or his approval. If anything, he found more and more things that were wrong, or imperfect.

> When we come to the end of ourselves, God is the only One we can turn to—and He's more than enough.

I tried to always look my best. I was never without makeup or beautiful clothes. That did not do anything for my husband. I read books to learn what I could do to get his approval. The more I tried, the more he rejected me.

We went to marriage counselors, five of them to be exact. It seemed to be the only way to get someone else's opinion of "why we could not get along." The counselors said the same thing, every time. One phrased it best: "Your husband has a cold steel beam running through him that no one can penetrate." I wanted to be accepted, allowed inside his steely exterior. After all, I was his wife and partner in life. I felt crazy inside, dejected, rejected, ugly, and unacceptable. I felt like a total failure in every way, so I tried to overcompensate in other ways by proving that I could be more successful than anyone else. Maybe that would help him accept and love me. I even remember thinking I had a mental problem, because the criticism was relentless. Nothing seemed to work. I prayed and tried to find a way out.

I even remember standing on a bridge thinking I could end it all right there, right then. But there was a child to consider. Life was miserable. Even though we seemed to have everything—a beautiful home, a beautiful child, we traveled the world, owned businesses, succeeded everywhere on the outside—we hid the disaster on the inside. What could I do to escape and not hurt anyone?

He started going to other cities for entertainment at gay bars since he didn't want anyone in town to know his secret. Our whole group of social friends seemed to change. I was totally lost and felt so threatened by the thought that "my husband is gay." Who could I talk to? I was scared, defeated, insecure, and miserable, but on the outside, no one knew. Truly, I lived in a prison, and I could find no escape. I had fixed all I could fix and I felt crazy on the inside. Again and again, I reminded myself that I was attractive, successful, and intelligent; however, I felt miserable. The continual criticism had begun to tear my spirit in two. All I could do was cry when I was alone. What a miserable and lonely place to be!

The nights became unbearable, and I began to sleep in a separate bedroom to try to keep from feeling the rejection. I would wake up and feel the loneliness overtake me. Somehow, I had to keep myself together for my young daughter, but she knew things were not right. The arguments and fights seemed to never end. This was not the life I had signed up for. I cried more than I laughed and I wanted out, to end the pain.

When I finally built up the courage to ask him if he was gay, his emotions seemed to explode. Of course, he denied having a problem. I knew we had a problem but he couldn't admit it. He threatened to have me committed to a mental institution because I was "acting so crazy." I realized I was beginning to believe his lies. That was the day I knew I had to get away from him, no matter the cost.

To survive and live a life that I had read about in God's Word, I was willing to leave everything. I wanted that more than success, more than things, more than friends—more than anything! One day while he was at work, I left with my daughter. Trusting God to show me how to rebuild my life at thirty-six years of age, I left everything behind. I never knew my father, and my mother had died when I was sixteen. There was no family to help me survive. God would be all I had.

After eighteen years of marriage, we divorced after a long and agonizing battle. Finally, I was free! My husband and I had always been believers, even youth counselors. Once we were divorced, I began to see the truth. I recognized the lies that had deceived me for so long. I was free!

In my search, I could not get close enough to God. He became my lifeline, my companion, my provision, my husband, my friend—my everything. Suddenly, it became real to me that I was actually an "OK" person, created in the image of God. I became free to be me and could finally smile. I could breathe and truly feel emotions that were not beaten down, but feelings of joy and peace that I had never known. It became apparent to me that the lies I had believed (that I was ugly, unacceptable, unpleasing) were lies from hell that had held me captive.

But this did not come overnight. It had been an eighteen-year journey into that prison and I had to slowly rebuild and learn to trust God in a new and fresh way. Suddenly, I felt like a person who could enjoy life, not a bleeding heart. I discovered I had real friends who accepted me just like I am, most of all, "Jesus"! What an incredible journey. I felt so thankful; I wanted to buy Bibles for everyone so they too could know the truth that would set them free.

As I began sharing my testimony of God's deliverance and provision when there was nothing else, I realized other women had been trapped in the same prison I had experienced. My testimony gave hope to other women as I became brave and free enough to share. The truth was being used to set others free! What an amazing transition took place. God was restoring my life in every area—socially, financially, emotionally, physically, and spiritually. What an incredible God we serve. I felt the love of God overtake my life and pervade everything I did.

> I felt the love of God overtake my life and pervade everything I did.

Today, I can barely remember the pain as I write my story. God has completely removed the pain from my heart! What an incredible healing has taken place, and as I share, it is like talking about some other person I once knew. God is an awesome God, and I am blessed more than I could ever ask or think today because He loves me!

Be blessed as you read this and know if He did it for me, He will do it for you.

## Becca's Story

My story is somewhat different than most, or so I thought. After my father's retirement from pastoring churches for forty years, he became severely depressed and spent his days in bed. He wouldn't talk to my mother or me, even though I tried to let him know that I loved him unconditionally. My mother and I watched his depression worsen so we checked him into a behavioral/psychiatric hospital. This would turn out to be one of the worst decisions of our lives.

During his counseling sessions, he shared that he had been involved with other men, on and off, since his teen years. Part of his therapy was to tell my mother about this part of his life. My mother then told my sister and me. During this time, he also tested positive for HIV. The doctors gave him very strong antidepressant drugs; however, four months later, he committed suicide.

I felt his entire life had been a lie. There were so many questions that would remain unanswered. As the oldest child, I had always been "Daddy's little girl" and I couldn't understand why he took the easy way out. Why couldn't he just deal with his problem? How could he have done this to me or my daughter—his only granddaughter? Didn't he love us? These questions plus many more have plagued me for years.

My parents' marital relationship of thirty-three years had always seemed strained. After his death, I wanted to blame my mother for his alternative lifestyle. If she had only been a more caring and loving wife, if...if.... I blamed my mother and then I blamed myself for not doing something, anything to prevent his suicide. I blamed myself for not making him realize how much he was loved. I blamed myself because he couldn't understand that we could get through it together, that he felt he couldn't share, that he felt unforgivable.

Then, I blamed God. How could He have allowed all of this? So much blame and no forgiveness were making me depressed. I didn't want to get out of bed or do anything. I started to go to counseling and would attend ladies meetings and retreats occasionally. I was prayed for time and time again. Things would improve for a while and then the negative emotions would come flooding over me again.

> I had unforgiveness in my life over things I didn't even realize I needed to forgive. But when I did, I was completely healed.

To make things worse, my mother did not want my sister or me sharing our family's "dirty little secret." This went on for over ten years. It was affecting my health. I developed serious problems in my legs.

Then I attended a ladies conference where Joan Hunter was ministering. The moment I met her, she could tell that I was in a lot of pain. She immediately prayed for me and my leg grew out. The pain was bearable but returned the next day. Joan knew there was more to my problem. That evening she ministered to me one-on-one. I dealt with the unforgiveness that I had toward my dad, my mom, God, and myself. I dealt with unforgiveness for things that I didn't even realize I needed to forgive.

The swelling in my leg went down and the pain was gone. I felt as if a tremendous weight had been lifted from me. I had a smile on my face. Everyone said that my countenance had changed.

I thank God that He brought Joan into my life.

# Angel's Story

As a registered nurse, I had been active in the medical community for my entire career, yet never understood the word *codependency*. Through the years, several friends had tried to talk to me about codependency, including giving me literature about Alcoholics Anonymous; however, I couldn't read it. I wouldn't…no, I *couldn't* admit that I was married to an alcoholic. I thought he just liked to drink and, occasionally, drank too much. He never suffered the effects of a hangover. After two or three hours' sleep, he was completely sober. He was very good at hiding the alcoholic effects from others; however, I could tell immediately when he had taken that first drink.

Embarrassing as it was, it became one of the many "secrets" we didn't talk about. Charming and fun, he was liked by everyone and made everybody laugh. No one would believe he had such a problem. He would help any- and everybody with anything they needed. However, when and if I needed something, I was ignored.

When we first met, my husband seemed to enjoy being with me, appreciate me, and truly love me. I wanted to please him. I can't pinpoint the time when my pleasing him started to become off balance, but it did. I gave, I gave, and I gave, but I never expected or demanded anything in return. I was willing to give my all to my spouse. Unfortunately, he didn't believe the same. We obviously didn't speak the same love language. He didn't believe in saying "I'm sorry." He didn't know how to say "thank-you" either.

Even though I had always been faithful to him, I was accused at least weekly, if not daily, of being interested in other men. If I was alone for more than ten minutes, he was sure I had been with someone else. To keep him quiet meant I had to have one of the children with me at all times as a chaperone. I wasn't allowed to talk to or about anyone of the opposite sex. To give someone an innocent hug meant a torrent of abusive accusations that would follow for weeks afterward.

> The journey may not be easy, but God is there to make it work for good if you trust in Him.

For seventeen years, I tried to make him happy. He was most attentive the first few years of our relationship; however, after he was sure I was under his control, his needs were always of number one importance. He was often sick with legitimate problems and ended up on disability for several years. The household income took quite a hit during those years; however, he still wanted to maintain his lifestyle and his needs had to be met. His money was his, and my income had to pay for everything else plus any extras he wanted, but could not afford. All I wanted was his loving attention.

To keep him happy, we went where he wanted to go, ate the food he wanted to eat, and drove the cars he wanted to drive. The only friends we socialized with were his friends. He didn't allow me to spend much time with my friends or family. I was under his control. I didn't have to ask specific permission to do things, but I knew from his look or stance whether I was doing something he thought was wrong. I knew better than to make him mad. His retaliation would come late at night while he was irrational and under the influence of alcohol. By morning he seemed to forget everything; and I wasn't about to start a conversation about what had happened the night before. Fear and frustration had me cornered.

Then, we got saved, he got healed, and we made a total commitment to God. I was ecstatic. He stopped drinking, and God worked through him in marvelous ways. We worked with various ministries, and I was sure our marriage was finally on the right track. After a few years, he started traveling more often and his jealous control returned. He would call me four or five times a day to check where I was and who I was with…starting at 8:00 a.m. and ending at 11:00 p.m. My fears isolated me. I often felt I was in prison and couldn't move or talk to anyone without his permission. As his traveling continued, it was apparent that his drinking had resumed, also. He was very successful with his work; however, his time at home was spent imbibing his alcohol.

One afternoon he came to my office, dropped some keys on my desk, and said, "Good-bye!" I wasn't sure what he meant, but had a bad feeling when he disappeared before I could ask anything. He had cleaned out the bank accounts and literally disappeared. Three weeks later, I found him in another state staying with friends. Like a dutiful wife, I dropped everything and rushed to his side to reconcile and save our marriage. Two weeks later, he decided to return home with me. Of course, all the money had been spent. No money, no job. His previous employer had a big heart and allowed his return to work. Our life returned to the old routine and habits.

Working in a ministry while smoking and drinking didn't paint a pretty picture. He wasn't going to admit to a problem, and he knew I wouldn't say anything, either. He was right. I closed my eyes and ignored his abusive behaviors. I was embarrassed that ministries trusted us to represent them and God while he was acting like that. I knew God would intervene sooner or later. I loved working in the ministry and was devastated at the thought of going back to the secular medical world again.

Indeed, our lives were turned upside down. His behaviors were revealed, and he lost his job. He again claimed he had no problem and chose to return to the world of carousing, drinking, and partying. Knowing what would happen, I declined his invitation to join him. He admitted to several affairs while he was traveling. I had no proof so I didn't know if he was telling the truth or just trying to hurt me.

We separated. He disappeared again. He left me with all the bills and a house that was more than I could handle. He took the car and left me with an old, barely functional truck. He hadn't let me drive a car for years, and suddenly, I had to drive a vehicle that wasn't dependable or safe. I had to return to the medical world again and worked long hours trying to make ends meet. They never met and the house went into foreclosure. Another embarrassment.

Was this journey easy? Far from it. I cried at the drop of a hat. I couldn't concentrate. I had to put on a "happy" face, a façade to hide my pain and pretend everything was great. "His going was for the best." It was for the best; however, I certainly didn't feel good. I worked, I ran, I biked, I swam, and I forced physical exertion so I wouldn't have to think. I didn't want to think about my "failure," didn't want to admit that my heart was bleeding and my life was a disaster. I had painted on a smile to hide the "secrets" for so long, very few people knew what went on behind closed doors when I was alone at night.

Not knowing what he was doing or what he could do to further affect the family, I knew a divorce was necessary. I didn't want to be held responsible for things he was doing or the bills he was incurring. I still loved him, but I knew I couldn't live with him anymore. I wouldn't return to that world. I had given my heart to Jesus and I wasn't going to take it back. To get a divorce meant papers would have to be served. I didn't have an address; I didn't know where he was. All I could do was pray. And God is always so faithful!

> I had given my heart to Jesus, and I wasn't going to take it back. All I could do was pray, and God was faithful.

I did locate him finally and we were divorced several years later. I still didn't understand what had happened to our marriage and felt I must have done something horrible to drive him back to the bottle. I picked up a book in a drugstore one day and read the back cover. Because I read at least two or three books a week, I am always looking for an interesting read. The few words on the back cover described my relationship with my husband perfectly. I bought the book and read it straight through. Ironically, it was a book a Christian friend had tried to give me years before.

I was given a crash course on codependency. I was crushed. I couldn't believe that I had been so blind. I thought I knew who I was and what I was doing in this life. I discovered the real me was hidden. My identity was totally wrapped up in my relationship to him. He controlled my thoughts, my speech, my actions, and my reactions to others. I was good at ignoring the negative, forgetting the bad, hiding the disgraceful, and smiling to hide all the "secrets."

The definition of a codependent was a perfect description of me. I was a "fixer." Our life had gone from one crisis to another and I always "fixed" things. The literature explained that women were prone to fall into this trap, along with those in the medical profession as well as Christians. Well, I hit a triple-header—I was all three. Of course, mothers want to "fix" things in the home, nurses want to help the sick get better, and Christians always want to share the good news and believe the best about everyone. I had been "fixing" things for so long; I didn't know how to change.

Even though we were no longer together, his expectations still controlled me. I couldn't ever say no to him. Thus, I couldn't say no to others, either. I worked longer hours than anyone else, more weeks without a break than anyone else. I had to be all things to all people. I wanted to make others happy and I did. I was very successful in my profession. I was called frequently for new, challenging, impossible situations that I handled efficiently and well. I was exhausted mentally, physically, and emotionally, but never felt I had done enough or been good enough. As long as I was "fixing" something for someone, I felt needed and wanted. I didn't know how to fix me!

I had to learn to say no!

We saw each other occasionally to discuss the children and other family issues. One day, I was late. A sense of panic overwhelmed me. "I'm late. He's going to be mad. What is he going to do to me this time? Oh, no! What am I going to do? I don't want to go through this again!" I had to stop, look at myself in the mirror, and have a serious chat with the one looking back at me. I didn't answer to him anymore. He could do nothing to me.

Research followed. I read every book I could find about codependency. After hours of prayer and study, I finally identified the path that my life had taken.

As a child I was very close to my father. We were together much of the time during my formative years. He was fifty years old when I was born and I was the apple of his eye. We had a great relationship, which continued until God called him home at age ninety-seven. We were best friends. He thought I was nearly perfect, which was difficult to live up to. I was not perfect; I just tried to be.

I grew up in church alongside my best friend, my dad. We went to every service plus extras held in town for special occasions. He was a committed man of God, from a family of missionaries and pastors, even though he had never been ordained. I knew that he prayed for me two or three times a day. His prayers covered me. Several times through the years, I came very close to total disaster. Only God's intervention saved me. I know my father's prayers surrounded me no matter how far I strayed. His respect and love for His God had a profound effect on God's reaction and protection over me.

Mother was another story. She was very secretive and spent most of her time with my older sisters and their problems. I tried very hard; however, I could never please her. Others would compliment me on the level of my work, my music, and my positive qualities. She ignored me. No hugs, no smiles, no compliments, no affirmation.

My research indicated the codependent behaviors often were passed from generation to generation. I was petrified that my children were going to follow the pattern. I found someone to help me break the generational curse over me and the children. Praise God, we are all free in Jesus. The children and their families are all committed to Him and are at peace. I had forgiven my husband for so much during the years; forgiving him one more time wasn't that difficult. This time I had the love of Jesus to help me. He died three years after the divorce, but that is another story.

> People don't always understand me, but Jesus does. My faith is not based on men, but on God.

In our small town, the "enemy" was never discussed or mentioned. No one was ever taught to rebuke him, bind him, or resist him. Once away from my home, the enemy did his thing. He drew me into the world. He enticed me away from small town mentality to big city sophistication. He clouded my mind and shrouded my childhood commitment to God with unreality and lies.

Satan distracted me, he fought for my soul, and he attempted to take my life. But *he lost!* Jesus won! My heavenly Father heard my earthly father's prayers and He answered them time and time again.

I gave, I did, I went, I came, I worked, I talked, I sang, I prayed. But I rarely spent quiet time to listen. I thought I had the answers when I didn't.

I committed my entire life to my spouse when I should have committed 100 percent to God.

I obeyed my husband implicitly when I should have obeyed God only.

I followed my husband too often when I should have followed God.

I made my husband my best friend when I should have given Jesus that ultimate privilege.

My faith is no longer based on man, but on God!

If God doesn't direct me to do something, I will do nothing.

If I don't have His peace about a situation, I wait for His direction.

When the enemy attacks, I stubbornly fight him, not the man being used by him.

People don't understand me, but my Father does.

When I need someone's arms around me, I curl up in my Father's lap.

When I get lonesome, I invite Jesus and the Holy Spirit into my home through praise and worship, mine as well as others' anointed CDs and DVDs.

When I want to see Jesus, I watch His servants minister to one another.

When I want to feel His love, I let Him love through me.

When I want a hug, I hug one of His hurting children.

Today, I am still codependent; however, that codependency is totally in relationship to God, not man.

No secrets, just Truth.

No pain, just Love.

Ultimate love.

Unconditional love.

Pure love that only He can give.

# Halley's Story

The most awesome evening in my life was August 28, 1996, the Wednesday night that I went running to the altar to rededicate my life to the Lord Jesus Christ. I have never been the same.

My journey to get there was a bumpy road. As a child I loved going to church. My favorite part was the singing and Sunday school. One Sunday the preacher gave a sermon on the short skirts and dresses the girls were wearing while he looked straight at the guilty young ladies. I decided if God was that judgmental then I did not want any part of church. I thought that God was a God of love and understanding. Isn't it ironic that I still prayed and believed God heard and answered me?

By the age of eleven, I had been sexually molested by my grandfather, father, and brother. The night my brother molested me, I asked God to never let him touch me again like that. The next day he drowned in a swimming accident. I remember telling myself to be careful of what I ask from God. I felt that I was the reason that he drowned, and I became fearful of God.

With no one I felt I could talk to, I buried what happened to me. Needless to say, I had a problem with male authority. I became very outspoken and stubborn at times. Then again I would turn inward and become an introvert. Through it all, I thought I was a normal girl.

By the age of thirteen, I started having sexual dreams. They all started out with a man and a woman, but would always end up with me being with a woman. This dream happened often. My first kiss was from a woman and felt safe and inviting. This is when I entered my lifestyle of lesbianism. Living that lifestyle until I was thirty-eight years old, I was in and out of relationships, never being content with one for very long. I was always searching for the one that would fulfill every need that I had. In my journey, I went looking everywhere for something that was missing in my life because I knew there had to be more. Hoping that I would find an answer, I had my palms read, went to people who channeled from the other side, and finally entered the new age movement, all to no avail. I found nothing to give me the answers to my unhappiness.

I went looking everywhere for something that was missing in my life because I knew there had to be more.

I got to a point in my life that I really did not want to live anymore. I had the pills to end my life, but when it got to the time to swallow them, I could not. My heart went out to my mother. How could she go through losing another child? So, I flushed the pills down the commode and decided suicide would never be a viable option.

I lived through two very serious automobile accidents without a scratch on my body, and an episode of carbon monoxide poisoning. That phrase "sex, drugs, and rock and roll" fit me perfectly. My favorite phrase was, "If it feels good, then do it." But again nothing fulfilled that void in my soul. I still needed something. But what, I did not know.

Before I went to sleep each Christmas Eve, I said a special prayer for my life. On December 24, 1995, I prayed that God would put someone spiritual in my life. He had been waiting patiently for that request. On the last day of that year, He answered that prayer. I met a wonderful woman at Foley's Women's Department. My sister and I were returning some clothes. In my lesbian mentality, I thought that she was interested in me so we started chatting. She asked me to go to church with her on New Year's Eve for a "celebration shut-in."

Rolling my eyes, I said, "Maybe next time." However, something compelled me to give her my phone number and told her to call me. My sister and I had been going to churches to see if we could find one that we liked. So I thought her invitation at that time was very interesting!

A week had passed and she had not called me so I went looking for her at Foley's. I found her. She had lost my phone number. I gave it to her again and asked her to call. Well, she did, and a friendship was born.

About 6:00 a.m. one Sunday morning she called and asked me, "What are you doing?"

I told her, "I am sleeping. What else do you do on Sunday morning?" She talked to me until she had me awake and told me her pastor's TV program was on at 7:00 a.m. if I wanted to watch him.

I told her, "Why not? There is nothing else on at that hour but church." Well, I did watch, and I liked what I saw. In fact, I liked it so much that I got up, got dressed, and was actually walking into the church as they started singing. I knew the moment that I walked in that church door that I had found what I was looking for. The pastor spoke right to my heart and the congregation showed me love when they acknowledged the newcomers.

Yes, I was home; however, I went to church for six months as a lesbian woman. I was more interested in what God was doing to my heart and soul. I wanted more and more from God. He knew it, and He was giving me what I wanted even though I did not always recognize it. I just knew that my soul was calm and at peace when I was at church. So I was there every time the doors were open. I could not get enough of God and His love, grace, and mercy. God just loved me all the time.

> I wanted more and more from God as He worked in my heart and soul.

About six months after I started attending church, I went to a women's conference. As I was walking up the sidewalk, I stopped, looked at my friend, and said, "I am no longer interested in women." I was in awe at the casualness of the statement, like it was nothing. It felt as if it was the most natural thing to come out of my mouth.

That statement nullified my entire adult life up to that moment. The most phenomenal thing was the peace that I felt. My God had let me walk in His love, grace, and mercy until I was ready. By His loving hand, He then delivered me from the lifestyle I had lived for so long. I have never looked back because there is nothing back there to look for or want to remember.

I am free, and whom the Son sets free is free indeed (John 8:36).

## Dawn's Story

Dawn Stefanowicz is a well-known author who lives in Toronto, Canada. She has written a book about her experiences growing up with a gay father. Her book is titled *Out from Under: Getting Clear of the Wreckage of a Sexually Disordered Home*. This is a portion of the preface of her book.[‡]

> The purpose in writing my book is to deliver an open, honest, and balanced account of what it was like growing up with a homosexual father and a weak, submissive mother. As a child, I struggled to deal with all the vivid and explicit sexual experiences, conflicts, and confusion I faced within this family setting.
>
> What makes my story unique is that I am willing to share the full story in my book—no holds barred. However, in doing so, I want to confirm my lasting love for my biological father. I will always love him. He has gone on before me to a better place, and I miss him very much. There are many times when I wish we could get together for a chat, share a light-hearted laugh, do something fun, or just quietly sit together.

---

[‡] Dawn Stefanowicz, *Out from Under: Getting Clear of the Wreckage of a Sexually Disordered Home*, preface. Used by permission. Dawn can be reached through her website at http://dawnstefanowicz.com.

As my father, he modeled and taught me a strong work ethic and business sense, and inculcated the sort of mature responsibility and endurance that makes it possible to overcome all adversity. He was not always proficient in all of these things. Even so, at times through reverse education—showing me how not to behave—he bequeathed to me a courageous resolve to live life honorably and to the fullest even through difficult circumstances. He set a high standard for me in his expectations of my career achievements. For this, I am truly thankful. He shared his cultural values, idealistic philosophies, moral reasoning, and personal life with me. He was my dad, and he will always be my father. I desire to share my own moments of joy as well as my struggles, pain, fear, and confusion in a manner that will broaden the understanding of the reader on how parents and family can affect their children.

I would not trade my father for any other. He did his best. He did not intend to hurt me by his life choices or deny me the opportunity of being genuinely loved. But, his attention and affection were often heavily influenced by his own neediness and preoccupation with the search for a father type who would love, affirm, and attend to him. He longed for and sought to obtain the sort of male companionship and love that he had never known as a child. But, as he sought to meet his own emotional needs through his gay lifestyle, the legitimate needs of his own children were often neglected or ignored. In recounting these incidents I have had to forgive my father again and again to avoid becoming enmeshed in bitterness, and have written out of a desire to achieve freedom through telling the truth, and to further my own emotional healing.

During my childhood, there were far too many lies told as I hid my personal life from others, and worried that I would offend not only my father but his partners and friends. I was concerned that my school friends and work mates would reject me if they knew about my father's numerous sexual partners and lifestyle. I have gone for years at a stretch telling hardly a soul about my deepest concerns and fears, and even now as I share my own story, I feel a sense of guilt, like I am betraying my parents and siblings in exposing family secrets. But, I have weighed the consequences of telling the truth against a higher purpose of shedding light on how parents and family structure can negatively impact children. In doing so I hope to encourage the development of a society in which all children live safely in families in which their best interests and needs are secured for them.

My father ultimately revealed how he came from a very dysfunctional family where sexual boundaries were violated, and incestuous relationships occurred. This dysfunction and trauma not only deeply affected his life, but also later, that of his family and children. Despite all this, my father had a strong spiritual background, which he shared with his children. Indeed he was involved in church work when he was younger. While he did not seem able or willing to follow biblical guidelines and admonitions in his own life, he did introduce his children to its teachings. Later as each of us struggled as best we could with the turmoil and confusion in our relationships and within our own lives, it was the faith and guidance provided by the Scriptures that helped me endure and even grow through these dark times in my life.

In closing I would like to quote Dr. Martin Luther King who said, "Our lives begin to end the day we become silent about things that matter." Certainly families and children matter. It is my hope that by sharing my experiences, readers in general, and those in position of influence and authority in particular, will be better informed in making decisions that may profoundly affect their families and their children, who are the hope and future of the next generation.

## Peter and Eleana

I want to tell you a testimony of what God did for me and my family.

Many years ago, I had an affair and cheated on my wife—not just an affair, but I moved in with another woman. My wife and the children were devasted. At the same time, I really didn't see anything wrong with what I had done and was doing.

After all, I am a CEO of a major company, and I supported them financially. I spent time with our children and took them to their games, all the while living with another women. I really couldn't comprehend why my wife didn't like the arrangement. She lacked for nothing—so I thought.

After several years of praying and standing in faith that we would reconcile, she gave up and filed for divorce.

God was dealing with me that this was not right and that I needed to return to my wife and family. My wife was praying for me to come home, also.

I told her I wanted to come home. At this time she was very hurt and said no. (I was still living with the other woman, and she didn't take me seriously.)

I couldn't understand why she said no. She had been praying for me to come home. I sought counsel from her pastor and told him the whole story. He advised me to get an apartment and get my life right with the Lord and then ask her again. He said that he would talk to my wife.

A few months later, after moving to an apartment, spending time with the Lord and praying, and sorting things in my life out, I asked her again.

She had been spending more time with the Lord, as well. During that time, she had asked God how she could ever forgive me for what I had done to her and the family. God showed her through Joan's teaching that what I had done was wrong and that it will always be wrong, but that she needed to forgive me, and by forgiving me, she would be released.

She forgave me that day. On the day the courts had set for the finalization of the divorce, I moved back in with the family. It has been several years, and we are leaders in our church and in the married couples department.

## Note from Joan

God hates divorce, but He loves the divorcee. I stood in faith for over thirteen years after I discovered my ex-husband was having an affair with another man. I prayed for him to change, and I knew that God could change him. But God will not override anyone's will. They have to be willing to change. Thank God, Peter was willing to submit his life to the Lord, and God restored their marriage.

## What Do You Need Today?

Did you see yourself in any of these scenarios? Could you empathize with the pain, frustration, and tears? Did you cheer when they finally reached victory?

Was I alone? Oh, no! Even though, at the time, I thought I was isolated, alone, and feeling pain no one else had ever felt. Thousands, perhaps more, are living through similar situations this very minute.

What do you need today? Do you need to get free? Or do you just need healing from a previous hurt, abuse, or attack?

I wasn't alone; I just felt that way. You aren't alone, either. Your answer is Jesus! Your victory is assured by His blood on the cross. He died for our complete healing, for our freedom, for our victory!

Choose Life! Choose Jesus!

What do you do next?

I sincerely suggest you go back to chapter five and follow through the steps listed there. Walk out your healing. Take the time to heal. Whether it takes days, weeks, or months, know that your total healing is coming.

No matter what you have or are going through, He is the answer. He will get you through any situation. This too will pass.

I pray these testimonies have blessed you, and I pray for this time in your life to go quickly.

And one day, you'll wake up and realize your memories feel like someone else lived them. You will remember the good parts of your previous relationships, not just the bad. You will be able to talk about them and minister to others to help them survive their nightmare, also.

What are you going to do? Help or hide?

You have the choice.

## Chapter 14

# Restoration!

## Can God Use Me?

Several years ago, after the divorce, I was traveling and ministering, partially with my parents and partially by myself. Several people commented or sent letters to me and my parents saying that God can't use me because I was divorced.

When I read some of these letters, I cried out to God asking, "Can You use *me*?"

"God, You saw people getting healed of pain, cancer, and other sicknesses, and yet they are telling me You can't use me."

In that still small voice of God's, through His Holy Spirit, I heard His response, "Just remember, they are not the one that called you. I am!"

## A Happy Ending

For many years, God laid it on my heart to write this book, all the while knowing that He would use my hurts and pain to help others. Not only to help them, but to give many others hope. Not just women, but men, too.

It took about seven years before I felt the timing was right. For many years, I kept saying, "I can't write the book until I live the last chapter."

I have and am living the last chapter, which is "Restoration." Unlike most books that just have a dedication page, this book has a dedication page and a dedication chapter—the final chapter. It is more of a thanksgiving chapter in that God has blessed me with a wonderful husband. One who loves God with *all* his heart and loves me with all his heart, also.

Kelley Murrell and I were married on December 12, 2004.

In preparation for the Houston Healing Explosion in the fall of 2004, I was teaching six healing schools at a church in the Houston area and invited other churches in the area to participate. For two years, Kelley had felt God calling him to the healing ministry, and he had a desire to learn more about healing. When I came to his church to invite them to participate, he knew this was for him. He started the next day. He attended all six schools.

I had hoped to remarry, but was leery of another relationship after the experiences with men in my life, especially in the area of desertion. From my natural father deserting me when I was an infant to other men making promises and not keeping them all throughout my life, a man in my life was the last thing that I expected to happen again.

Kelley asked me to go out with him on the weekend. Because of my busy traveling schedule, I told him I wouldn't be free on a weekend for several weeks. He said he would wait as long as he had to. I later told him a Wednesday or Thursday evening would be available sooner. We met at church and went out as a group. Then we started meeting at restaurants. When I felt comfortable enough to have him come to my home and know where I lived, he came to pick me up for our evenings out. We had a great time getting to know one another.

After the Healing Explosion, I was scheduled to have a root canal looked at by an oral surgeon. I had had problems with that tooth for years. Kelley offered to take the day off and accompany me. Since the procedure was done under general anesthesia, I had to have someone to take me home. I don't come out of anesthesia very easily.

While I was in surgery, he sat in the lobby and read his Bible. After a long period of time, the doctor came out to tell him that I was okay and that they had to remove a cyst the size of a golf ball. He was very concerned. He took me home after a few hours of recovery at the doctor's office and helped me to the couch where I lay down and fell asleep again. I remember waking up in my groggy condition and seeing him sitting on the floor right next to the couch, but more importantly, right next to me reading his Bible.

*I knew he would never leave me!*

I realized at that moment, he would never leave me. In sickness or in health, in good times or bad, we would be together. At that moment, I realized he was the one God had sent to me to love me and take care of me the rest of my life.

Two days later he asked me to marry him (swollen face and all) and I said, "Yes!"

I had prayed for a man who would love me for me—not for who I was in the world's eyes, but for *me*—one who would never leave me nor forsake me. A man who would be faithful to the vows that he made to me. A man who would not turn his back on God. A man who had lived a pure life. A man who would be faithful to me.

Kelley is all of that and more.

During trips when he is unable to accompany me, I could not minister effectively if I wondered about what he was doing, and who he was doing it with. I have great peace when I am traveling because I know he is reading the Word and praying, especially for me. That is very comforting.

Many have said to me, "Weren't you afraid that he might be like your ex-husband or other men in your life?" God gave me this Scripture:

> *There is no fear in love; but perfect love casts out fear, because fear involves torment. But he who fears has not been made perfect in love.* (1 John 4:18)

Where perfect love is concerned, there is no fear. You can be married with children and still be lonely. I pray for you right now that He will take the loneliness away, in Jesus' name. I speak blessings on all your relationships. Especially your relationship with God.

One of the greatest rewards through my story is my children. One day, one of my daughters made this remark, which overwhelmed me with love and tears:

> *Mom, in the school of hard knocks you graduated valedictorian. I am very proud of you that you made it through this time. Not only that you made it through, but you have been an example in your relationship with God and that has never wavered. It has been a tremendous example to me and my sisters.*

As I close this book, allow me to pray for you:

Father, I pray for everyone who has read this book. I pray they have been blessed and that their hearts have been healed. Father God, I pray that You remove all fear from this person and that what happened will never happen again. I pray for peace in both their life and heart. Father, I pray that through this book and especially this final chapter, You will give them hope. Hope for a brighter future...hope of a future.

Father, I pray for the one who is feeling lonely. If they are single and want to get married, that You would guide them to do whatever they can do to prepare for the one You want to send to them. Father, prepare that perfect person. Father, I know You are always with us and we are never alone.

Father, I pray happiness over this person, in Jesus' name. I know a mate cannot make anyone happy. Only You can bring true happiness, Father. We give You our hearts and lives anew, Father, knowing You have great and special plans for the days ahead. You will bring special people into our lives and we wait with our expectors up and ready, Father. We will be very careful to give You all the glory, in Jesus' name.

*I AM FREE!        I AM LOVED!*

*I AM HEALED!   I AM BEAUTIFUL!   I AM VALUABLE!*

*I AM DELIVERED! I AM TOTALLY FORGIVEN! I AM A GIVER!*

*I AM A WHOLE NEW PERSON!   I AM GOD'S FAVORITE!*

*THANK YOU, JESUS!   HALLELUJAH!*

*IN HIS LOVE,*

*~JOAN*

# About the Author

t would be difficult to describe Joan Hunter in one word. How can you take all the signs and wonders that occur in her services and place that on paper? You can't...

Joan Hunter has been involved in the healing ministry for over thirty years. Along with her parents, Charles and Frances Hunter, she has ministered to thousands of people in the area of physical healings. She has traveled the world laying hands on the sick and seeing them recover. God has expanded her ministry to include total healing—body, soul, and spirit. She is also the author of *Healing the Whole Man Handbook.*

She is married to Kelley Murrell and lives in Kingwood, Texas. She has four grown daughters, four stepsons, and is a grandmother. She co-pastored a church in Dallas for eighteen years until 1999. This gives her a wide range of experience in the ministry.

God has healed Joan in every area of her life. She encourages others that they can lay hands on the sick and see them recover. The healing power of God is not reserved for just a few...but for those who believe. Joan encourages you not to give up on your dreams and visions, but to fulfill your destiny that God has for you.

Four of my blessings

Left to Right: Abigail, Melody, Spice, Charity

As I looked at this picture and what He has done for my family—
not just my girls, but my family—I am so appreciative of how He has
healed me and is healing them.

Left to Right: Chris and Abigail, Nathan and Spice, Melody,
Charity and Ted and their son, Luke

Joan and Kelley

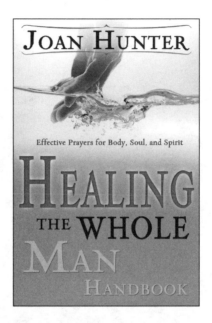

## Healing the Whole Man Handbook:
## Effective Prayers for Body, Soul, and Spirit
*Joan Hunter*

You can walk in divine health and healing. The secrets to God's words for healing and recovery are in this comprehensive, easy-to-follow guidebook containing powerful healing prayers that cover everything from abuse to yeast infections and everything in between.

Truly anointed with the gifts of healing, Joan Hunter has over thirty years of experience praying for the sick and brokenhearted and seeing them healed and set free. By following these step-by-step instructions and claiming God's promises, you can be healed, set free, and made totally whole—body, soul, and spirit!

ISBN: 978-0-88368-815-8 • Trade • 240 pages

WHITAKER
HOUSE

www.whitakerhouse.com